THE GOURMET'S COMPANION

Curious Fables, Facts and Folklore
from the World of Food and Drink

Ross Leckie

THE GOURMET'S COMPANION

Ross Leckie

First published in the United Kingdom by The Edinburgh Publishing Company Limited, Admiral House, 30 Maritime Street, Leith, Edinburgh, Scotland EH6 6SE.

British Library Cataloguing-in-Publication Data.
A catalogue record for this book is available from the British Library.

ISBN 1 872401 17 X

Cover illustration: The Roast Beef of Olde England by Hogarth, kind permission of the Tate Gallery, London.

Printed and bound in the United Kingdom by Inglis Allen, Scotland

ABOUT THE AUTHOR

Ross Leckie read classics at Oxford and worked variously as a roughneck on North Sea oil rigs, as a schoolmaster and as a director of a major insurance company. He is a regular commentator on Scottish affairs on television and radio and has contributed to, amongst others, *The Scotsman*, *The Times* and *The Spectator* and has a regular column in *The Oldie*. He is a prolific writer whose published works include *Tears of Things (Collected Poems)* 1988; *Bluff Your Way in the Classics* 1989 (now in its third edition) and *Grampian, A Country in Miniature 1991*. He has an absorbing passion for, and an encyclopædic historical knowledge of good food and drink, both of which he is said to enjoy, especially when he isn't paying.

CONTENTS

DEDICATION

To Sophie on the one hand; mince and tatties on the other.

INTRODUCTION

Food, said the chicken to the egg, is as old as life. Good food is one of man's greatest joys and hunger one of his greatest fears. Food is indeed the foundation of civilisation, marked in the beginning by the cultivation of crops and the domestication of animals. For as soon as early man gave up the nomadic life in pursuit of the wild animals on which he fed and became, instead, a pastoralist, civilization began. Settled crops, stocks and stores of food and full stomachs were the fundaments of society. The stomach is an instrument of culture as important as the brain.

Food has remained a crucial force in shaping the course of history. Emigrations from the Near East in search of pasture brought civilisation to Europe. Ancient Greece and Rome both grew great by colonising land to feed their people. Food as much as religion was the cause of the Crusades as our ancestors sought to re-open ancient spice routes to the East, closed by the expansion of Islam. Spices were the measure of wealth in the Middle Ages, so coveted that Columbus died disgraced for having found only gold in the Americas and not the spices he had promised, and so treasured that mediæval potentates kept their spice chests locked beside them.

So today food is still a potent force, if a madder one. Excess in the west - obesity and EEC food mountains - is marked by shocking want elsewhere and neither prayer, precept, BandAid and certainly not politicians, it seems, can do anything about it.

Most of us who read this book will, mercifully, never have been or ever will be hungry. But if we're full of food, I hope we don't have to be pompous. Food should be fun, if you have it. This book tries to demonstrate some of that fun in the hope that, one day, the great common denominator of food will be available to and enjoyed by all.

Ross Leckie

The sense of taste is the most exquisite of all.

- Cicero, 106-43 B.C.

"An epicure", Thomas
Rowlandson.

ON THIS DAY IN JANUARY...

3rd January 1350
- A proclamation prohibits the rearing of pigs within the city of Paris and authorises the police to kill pigs on sight, keeping the heads as a perquisite.

9th January 1379
- King James I of Castile founds the knightly Order of the Pigeon for faithful husbands. Only the first of its planned annual banquets is held, for want of suitably monogamous members.

11th January 1935
- The great French gourmet Henri Babinsky, alias "Ali-Bab", dies in Paris, not long after the publication of his study of obesity among gourmands.

The gourmet is often confused with the gourmand - understandably, since only a fine but important line divides them. Both words have French roots. The gourmand is one whose principal pleasure in life is eating and drinking, often to excess. The gourmet, however, is a connoisseur of good food and wines. A gourmand's main interest is quantity, a gourmet's, by contrast, quality.

THE GASTRONOME

A gastronome is a gourmet with pretensions. Both in French and in English, the word came into use only in the 19th century and comes from the Greek for the law of the stomach. Gastronomy, the art and science of delicate eating, is not to be confused with the much older gastromancy, the art of divination by the belly, whereby the ancient Greeks and then the Romans used to "read" the entrails of a sacrifice before deciding, for example, whether or not to get out of bed in the morning. Although gastromancy has rather died out, there are times when one wishes that modern economists and politicians might revive it.

The pretentious gourmet might prefer to style himself a *gastrosoph*, one who is skilled in matters of eating. The gourmand might prefer the noun *gastrophile*, one who loves his stomach, or even *gastrolater*, a "belly-worshipper". This might entail, however, severe *gastrodnia*, pain in the stomach, ore even *gastralgia*, neuralgia of the stomach.

Anyway the "gasts-" might hope to count amongst their friends a *gastrophilanthropist*, a "benevolent purveyor for the appetites of others". It doesn't much matter, as long as such "gasts-" don't get carried away and take up *gastrotomy*, the cutting open of the stomach, or *gastrorrhaphy*, the suture of wounds in the abdomen Those who are that desperate could always ingest "Complan" instead.

"Three men at table and a cook", Thomas Rowlandson.

A man hath no better thing under the sun,
than to eat, and to drink, and to be merry.
                              - Ecclesiates 8.15.

"Scottifying the palate at Leith",
Thomas Rowlandson.

ON THIS DAY IN JANUARY...

12th January 1571
- The Corporation of Spice-bread Makers of Reims, after years of schism, breaks away from the Corporation of Pastrycooks & Wafer-makers. Its coat of arms has been wafer-less ever since.

14th January 1493
- Christopher Columbus, describing the island of Hispaniola (now Haiti) provides our first mention of the chilli, a "better spice than our pepper (*mejor que pimienta nuestra*)".

15th January 1920
- Prohibition is imposed on the citizens of the United States.

The gourmet in need of a change can always style himself an *epicure*, one who "cultivates a refined taste for the pleasures of the table", and dismiss roundly those who believe an epicure to be merely a sensual glutton. Poor Epicurus, a Greek philosopher of the 4th century B.C., has always had a bad press. His contemporaries mistrusted him because he lived in a latter-day commune which included slaves and women. That was definitely not on. In fact Epicurus was a man of learning and discernment who took his pleasures seriously, not wantonly. "We say that pleasure is the beginning and end of living happily", said Epicurus. But he sought to avoid those pleasures which involve subsequent pain. Pleasure he argued, is not be found in satisfying desires, but in the state of having had desires satisfied. A modern epicure should wear the designation with pride.

AMPHITYRON

If people want a derogatory term for a glutton, they have it in *Amphitryon*. When and if he was alive, Amphitryon was foster-father to Hercules. The French playwright Molière (1622-73) borrowed him from Greek myth to act as host of a great and comic dinner in a play of the same name. So did the word come into English as denoting a gluttonous host. Anyway, you may safely call someone you rather dislike a "veritable Amphitryon". Since you are almost certain not to be understood, you are unlikely to offend. You could even try "amphivorous Amphitryon", an Amphitryon who eats both animal and vegetable matter. Refer knowledgeably to the great Grimod de la Reyniérè's *Manuel des amphitryons* (1808), which defines the rules of behaviour at table, and Maurice des Ombiaux's *L'Amphitryon d'aujourd'hui* (1936) which does it again.

"Disappointed epicures", Thomas Rowlandson.

Cookery means... English thoroughness,
French art and Arabian hospitality; it means
the knowledge of all the fruits and herbs and
balms and spices; it means carefulness,
inventiveness and watchfulness.
                    - John Ruskin, 1819-1900.

"At least we won't have to go to the circus!"

ON THIS DAY IN JANUARY...

16th January 1660
- Sieur Audiger returns from Genoa to France and presents Louis XIV with a hamper of green peas, to the astonishment and delight of the whole court.

16th January 1870
- During the siege of Paris, the Café Anglais offers braised elephants' feet with ham, spices, garlic and Madeira. The unfortunate elephants came from the local zoo.

16th January 1991
- The Hyatt Regency Hotel in Guadalajara, Mexico presents to the world a loaf of bread, *Rosca de Reyes*, that is 3,491 feet and 9 inches long.

"Oysters are more beautiful than religion", thought Saki (H.H. Munro). He can't have been reading the entry in the 1911 edition of *The Encyclopædia Britannica*:

"The pair of ganglia near the mouth, variously called labial or cerebral, represent the cerebral pair and pleural pair of a gastropod combined, and the parieto-splanchnic pair correspond to the visceral ganglia, the commissure which connects them with the cerebro-pleural representing the visceral commissure. Each of the visceral ganglia is connected or combined with an olfactory ganglion underlying an area of specialised epithelium, which constitutes the olfactory organ, the osphradium".

Most gourmets would be well advised to forget all this and get on with enjoying their oysters, as long as they remember never to eat one unless there's an "R" in the month- especially now that the native British oyster is staging a comeback against their Pacific bretheren which can be eaten all year round. The pRudent, then, only eat oysters between September and April. In England and Scotland, however, the legally "close time" for oysters is only 15th June to 4th August.

The wealthy gourmet might follow the proverb "Who eats oysters on St. James's Day (July 25th) will never want". Oysters obtainable so unseasonably must have come from far away and be, therefore, expensive, even if they haven't come as far as from Lewis Carroll:

"The Walrus and the Carpenter
Walked on a mile or so,
And then they rested on a rock
Conveniently low:
And all the little oysters stood
And waited in a row.

'The time has come', the Walrus said,
'To talk of many things:
Of shoes - and ships - and sealing wax -
Of Cabbages - and Kings...'"

Some early nineteenth century gourmets eating oysters, by L. Boilly, 1825.

Epicurean cooks sharpen with cloyless
sauces his appetite.
            -William Shakespeare, 1564-1616,
                  Antony & Cleopatra, II.1

"I wish he'd go to the theatre!"

ON THIS DAY IN JANUARY...

18th January 1920
- The world's largest single vine is uprooted, having been planted in California in 1842. It has consistently yielded more than nine tons of grapes a year.

19th January 1894
- Lobster Thermidor is created for the first time at Mairie's, a famous Paris restaurant, on the evening of the première of a play called *Thermidor*.

21st January 1555
 - The astrologer Nostradamus publishes a cookery book, the *Excellent et Moult Utile Opuscule (The Excellent and Very Useful Little Work)*.

In ancient Greek mythology Tereus, King of Thebes, married the princess Prokne. But when he saw her sister Philomela, he fell violently in love with her and raped her. To prevent Philomela from telling Prokne, Tereus cut out her tongue and hid her away. But Philomela embroidered an account of her woes on a piece of needle-work and managed to send it to her sister. In revenge, Prokne killed her son Itys and served him up at a banquet to his father.

SUPPOSED RECONCILIATION

Atreus, King of Mycenae, had a beautiful wife called Aerope. His brother Thyestes raped her. Atreus pretended to forgive, but killed Thyestes' children and served them to his brother as the main dish in a banquet of supposed reconciliation.

Damocles was a courtier to King Dionysius (430-367 B.C.) who annoyed the king with his fulsome praise. To show Damocles what power was really like, Dionysius organised a great feast at which Damocles was the principal guest. Above his chair was a sword, hanging from the ceiling by a thin thread.

The Aztec worship of the god of war, Huitzilopochtli, involved his servants feasting on the bodies of their prisoners.

FISH FODDER

During the reign of the Roman emperor Augustus, epicures vied with one another in the quality of the fish they served at their banquets. The turbot, reared in ponds and lakes in sumptuous Roman gardens, was especially prized. One Roman knight, Vedius Pollio, went so far as to feed his turbot on the bodies of his human slaves, thrown alive to the fish.

"The rape of Lucrece",
Thomas Rowlandson.

A wonderful bird is the pelican,
His bill will hold more than his belican.
He can take in his beak food enough for a week,
But I'm damned if I see how the helican.
                          - D. L. Merritt.

ON THIS DAY IN JAN/FEB...

25th January 1759
- Birth of the Scottish poet Robert Burns. Burns Night, at which haggis is eaten and much whisky drunk, is celebrated at dinners throughout the world.

26th January 1900
- Launch of the first *Michelin* guide to the restaurants of France. Its antecedents lie in such guides to amenities for itinerant medieval pilgrims as Picard's 1150 *Liber Sancti Jacobi*.

2nd February 1492
- First celebration of the feast of Candlemas, following an edict by Pope Gelasius I.

John, 10th Earl of Sutherland, had a cousin, Lady Isobel Sinclair, who was desperate for the earldom to pass to her own son. So, on 18th June 1567, she tried to poison John, his pregnant wife Marion and their son Alexander at a dinner in Helmsdale Castle on Scotland's north-east coast. The Earl drank poisoned wine that Isabel had prepared. Knowing he was dying, John rose and with his last reserves of will pulled the tablecloth from the table, scattering the meal and thereby saving his son and successor.

A FUNERAL FEAST

A French gourmet once gave a funeral feast, recorded in Huysmans' book *Against Nature*:

"The dining-room, draped in black, opened out onto a garden whose paths had been strewn with charcoal for the occasion; the garden pond had been edged with black basalt and filled with ink; the shrubberies replanted with cypresses and pines. Dinner was served on a black cloth. While a hidden orchestra played funeral marches, the guests were waited on by naked negresses and dined off black plates. The fare consisted of turtle soup, Russian rye bread, black olives, caviare, mullet botargo, black pudding, game served in sauces the colour of liquorice, chocolate creams, mulberries and black-heart cherries. From dark-tinted glasses, the guests drank the wines of Oporto. After coffee, they enjoyed kvass, porter and stout. On the invitations, the dinner was described as a funeral banquet in memory of the host's virility, lately but only temporarily deceased."

"Banquet for two".

To invite someone to be our guest is to
undertake responsibility for his happiness
all the time he is under our roof.
  - Jean-Anthelme Brillat-Savarin, 1755-1826.

From Rowlandson's "Comparative
Anatomy".

ON THIS DAY IN FEBRUARY...

4th February 1850
- Birth of César Ritz, the son of a Swiss shepherd, who lives to establish the unrivalled reputation of Claridge's and the Hyde Park Hotel before opening the London Ritz in 1906.

6th February 1770
- First formal restaurant in western Europe opens: the "Champ d'Oiseau" in Paris' Rue des Poulies.

7th February 1991
- A model made of chocolate in the shape of a Spanish sailing ship and weighing 8,818 pounds, 6 ounces is exhibited in Barcelona.

A WEDDING FEAST

Cervantes' (1547-1616) *Don Quixote* describes as follows the wedding feast of a wealthy farmer, Camacho:

"There was a whole ox spitted on the trunk of an elm and, in the hearth over which it was to roast, there was a fair mountain of wood burning. Six earthern pots were arranged around this blaze... Whole sheep disappeared within them as if they were pigeons. Innumerable skinned hares and plucked chickens were soon to be swallowed up in these pots. Birds and game of all kinds were also hanging from the branches... There were piles of white loaves, like heaps of wheat in barns. Cheeses, built up like bricks, formed walls and two cauldrons of oil, bigger than dyers' vats, were used for frying pastries, which were lifted out with two sturdy shovels and then plunged into a cauldron of honey".

"Banquet", Philipp Gulle.

So it is that the expression *noces de Gamache* (Camacho's wedding) has come to mean a sumptuous feast costing an enormous amount of money. A similar expression is *Trimalcio's Feast*, after the character created by the Roman writer of the first century A.D., Petronius. Trimalcio offers his friends a gargantuan banquet which includes fish, plump chickens, wild boars, sows' udders, pigs stuffed with sausages and black puddings, oysters and snails.

The Roman Emperor Heliogabalus (204-222) was a notorious sybarite, especially inclined to culinary excess. His particular pleasure was to organise day-long meals in the course of which different courses were served at different houses throughout Rome. For one banquet, preceded by a mock naval battle on canals filled with wine, he ordered 600 ostrich brains as an hors d'oeuvre.

Happy are the inhabitants of Bordeaux, for whom living and drinking are one and the same!

- Ausonius, 310-395 A.D.

"I'd like one out of that bowl this time."

ON THIS DAY IN FEBRUARY...

7th February 1969

- Charles Winfield of Texas consumes 210 live goldfish at one sitting.

12th February 12

- The Roman gourmet Apicius bids 5,000 sestertii (in modern terms, around £5,000) for one fish, a rare red mullet weighing 4 pounds.

12th February 1876

- Daniel Peter, a Swiss confectioner, invents solid milk chocolate with the help of Henri Nestle's new dried milk.

The 5th century Roman historian Macrobius describes a run-of-the-mill supper given in Rome by the aristocrat Lentullus:

"The first course was composed of sea-hedgehogs, raw oysters in abundance, all sorts of shellfish, and asparagus. The second comprised a fine fatted pullet, a fresh dish of oysters, and other shellfish, different kinds of dates, univalvular shellfish (as whelks, conchs and so on), more oysters, but of different kinds, sea-nettels, beccaficoes, chines of roebuck and wild boar, fowls covered with a perfumed paste, a second dish of shellfish and purples - a very costly kind of crustacea. The third and last course presented several hors d'oeuvre, a wild boar's head, fish, a second set of hors d'oeuvre, ducks, potted river fish, leverets, roast fowls, and cakes from the marshes of Ancona".

A SWAN SOIRÉE

One of the more unusual prerogatives of the British royal family is the swan (*Cygnus olor*), the right to which was first assumed by King John as the 12th century turned. Swan in general and cygnet in particular was considered a great delicacy, especially if the cygnets had been fattened on oats to remove any fishy taste. Henry III was especially fond of the bird. He ordered his sheriffs to provide him with 125 of them for his Christmas feast in 1251. It came to be the case that no loyal subject could possess a swan without a licence from the Crown. So did every swan in a "game" (the old legal term) have to bear on its bill a distinguishing mark of ownership or *cygninota*. By the reign of Queen Elizabeth I, more than 900 swan-marks were recognised by the royal swanherd, whose authority over all the swans in the kingdom was absolute.

Here, perhaps, is a calling for passed-over politicians.

"Leda and the swan", Thomas Rowlandson.

In this island, there are many spices... their Highnesses may see that I shall give them all the gold they require, spices also and cotton, mastic and aloes. I think also I have found rhubarb and cinnamon.
   - Christopher Columbus anchored off the West Indies, 15.02.1493.

From Rowlandson's "Comparative Anatomy".

ON THIS DAY IN FEBRUARY...

14th February 162 B.C.
- In order to save grain, the Lex Faunia forbids Romans from eating fattened hens. The chicken breeders get round the law by fattening capons, castrated cockerels, instead.

17th February 1800
- The last week of the siege of Genoa by Messena begins. All the Genoans have left to eat is fifty tons of almonds.

19th February 1409
- John the Fearless, Duke of Burgundy, institutes the Order of the Hop. Its motto was "Ich Zuighe", meaning in Flemish "I savour".

The Roman knight Geta gave banquets at which there was a course for each letter of the alphabet. As if that wasn't enough, he further insisted that each of these courses should contain all the meats whose name began with that letter!

UNUSUAL ENTERTAINMENT

In 1237, at the marriage of Robert, son of Saint-Louis, to Machault, Countess of Artois, guests enjoyed unusual entertainments between each course. A horseman crossed the banqueting hall, making his horse walk on a thick rope suspended above the guests' heads. At the four corners of the table were musicians seated on oxen. The harpists were dressed as monkeys and sat on tethered living goats.

"Les Fetes Saturnales".

In 1470, the Earl of Warwick gave a banquet to celebrate the installation of the Archbishop of York. Papers found in the Tower of London list the raw ingredients: 300 quarters of wheat, 300 tuns of ale, 104 tuns of wine, 10 fat oxen, 6 wild bulls, 300 pigs, 1,004 sheep, 3,000 calves, 100 peacocks, 200 cranes, 8 seals, 4 porpoises, 300 bream, 300 pikes, 4,000 pigeons, 4,000 rabbits, 4,000 ducks, 204 bitterns, 500 partridges, 5,000 woodcock, 400 plovers, 100 quails, 100 curlews, 4,000 bucks, roebucks and does, 200 pheasants, 4,000 cold venison pasties and much, much more. No wonder taxes were so high!

1,286 MASTERPIECES

When King Henri III of France visited Venice, the city prepared an unusual banquet in his honour. Everything was made of spun sugar: the bread, plates, knives, forks, tablecloth, napkins and hundreds of table decorations. The famous master craftsman Nicolo delle Cavalliera had created 1,286 masterpieces.

*He who does not mind his belly will hardly
mind anything else.*
                    - Samuel Johnson, 1709-84.

*"Behaviour at table",
Thomas Rowlandson.*

ON THIS DAY IN FEB/MAR...

22nd February 1877

- Equipped with refrigeration machines designed by Ferdinand Carré, the ship *Paraguay* and 80 tons of meat leave Buenos Aires for France. Despite the ship's running aground off the coast of Senegal and being delayed for two months, the meat reaches Le Havre in perfect condition.

23rd February 1820

- Frederick Accum publishes his *Treatise on Adulterations of Food and Culinary Poisons*. It leads, eventually, to the first English Pure Food Laws in the 1860s.

26th February 1604

- Ravioli first appear in a menu, "for sale at the sign of the Golden Fleece, near the church of the eleven thousand virgins", according to Lancelot de Casteau of Mons, chef to three princes of Liège.

In upper-class Edwardian England, what would seem to us a fabulous feast was but normal. A best-seller of the time, *The Manners of Polite Society*, subtitled *Complete Etiquette for Ladies, Gentlemen and Families*, records a typical dinner:

"The table was set for twenty-six and standing on it were elegant gilt candelabra. In the middle of the table was a magnificent plateau of gold, flowers surmounted the summit, and the circular stages below were covered with confectionary, elegantly arranged. On each side were tall china fruit baskets, in the centre of each immense pine-apples of hot-house growth. Down each side of the whole long table were placed large, round, saucer-shaped fruit dishes, heaped up with peaches, plums, pears, nectarines... Alternating with the fruit were all the *entremets* or French dishes in covered dishes. All the plate was superb. The dinner set was of French china, gilt and painted with roses. The sideboard held only the show silver and the wine.

Each servant handed the dishes in his white kid gloves, and with a damask napkin under his thumb. They offered a plate of soup to each guest. After the soup, Hock and Mosselle were offered. A dish of fish was then placed at each end of the table - one was salmon, the other turbot. Directly after the fish came the *entremets*. The wine following the fish was Madeira and sherry.

Afterwards a saddle of Welsh mutton was placed at the master's end of the table, and at the lady's end a boiled turkey. The poultry was not dissected - nothing being helped but the breast. Ham and tongue was then supplied. Next came the vegetables. Next, two dishes of game were put on. Then placed along the table were the sweet things - Charlottes, jellies, frozen fruits etc. A lobster salad was put on with the sweets. On a side-table were Stilton and cream cheese, to be eaten with the salad. After this, port wine - the Champagne being early in the dinner.

After sitting awhile over the fruit, the lady of the house gives the signal by looking and bowing to the ladies on each side. The gentlemen all rise and remain standing while the ladies depart. The servants then all retire, except the butler, who remains to wait on the gentlemen while they linger awhile (not more than a quarter of an hour) over the fruit and wine".

"Le Souper Fin",
J.S. Helman after Moreau.

Sire, I have greater need of cooking pots than of instructions.
- **The statesman Talleyrand, 1754-1838, to Louis XVIII before the Congress of Vienna.**

A banquet.

ON THIS DAY IN MARCH...

1st March 1726
- Four thieves are arrested for robbing corpses during the plague of Marseilles. Their immunity to the disease that kills their victims is explained by their wearing masks soaked in a mixture of garlic and vinegar.

2nd March 1602
- The Dutch East India Company is founded.

3rd March 1603
- In his journal for this day, Champlain, the founder of Quebec, mentions "roots cultivated by the Indians, which have the flavour of the artichoke". He has discovered the Jerusalem artichoke.

October 1971 was the 2,500th anniversary of imperial Iran. To mark the occasion, the Shah organised in Persepolis the most lavish banquet in history. It lasted for 5 hours. The menu comprised quails' eggs stuffed with Iranian caviar, a mousse of crayfish tails in Nantua sauce, stuffed rack of roast lamb, roast peacock stuffed with *foie gras*, fig rings and raspberry and champagne sherbet. Amongst the wines served was *Chateau Lafite-Rothschild* 1945 at £45 (now £235) per bottle, delivered by Maxime's of Paris.

WHEN THE WINE TURNED TO ICE

Mount Huascaran in Peru is 22,205 feet high. This did not deter nine Australian gourmet climbers who, on 28th June 1989, held a select dinner party on the summit. They had carried with them a table, chairs, wine and a three course meal. All went well, save for the fact that the wine turned to ice.

In 1746, Sir Edward Russell, Commander in Chief of the British armed forces, gave a small drinks party for a few of his closest friends. Punch was served from a massive marble basin filled with four barrels of brandy and eight of water, twenty-five thousand lemons, eighty pints of lemon juice, thirteen hundred weight of sugar, five pounds of nutmeg, three hundred biscuits and a pipe of Malaga wine. In a little rose-wood boat, a cabin boy rowed about on the surface of the punch, serving the six thousand guests.

"A hunt supper", Thomas Rowlandson.

*My definition of Man is, a "Cooking
Animal". The beasts have memory,
judgement, and all the facilities and
passions of our mind... but no beast is a
cook.*

- Samuel Johnson, 1709-84.

*"The triumph of sentiment",
Thomas Rowlandson.*

ON THIS DAY IN MARCH...

6th March 1870
- Alexandre Dumas, author of *The Three Musketeers*, completes his monumental *Grand Dictionnaire de Cuisine*, a work of 1,152 pages.

8th March 1774
- Calling her the "fresh pork of my thoughts", the Marquis de Sade writes to his wife from prison with requests for food.

12th March 1690
- A German naturalist, Engelbert Kaempfer, publishes his *Geschichte und Beschreibung von Japan*, an account of his travels and gastronomical adventures in Japan. So is Japanese cuisine first introduced to the West.

Grimod de La Reynièrè was arguably the greatest gourmet France has ever produced. He died on Christmas Eve, 1837, leaving as his last will and testament the following recipe for *"an unparalleled roast"*, punctuated with references to actresses of his time:

"Stuff an olive with capers and anchovies and put it in a garden warbler. Put the warbler in an ortalan, the ortalan in a lark, the lark in a thrush, the thrush in a quail, the quail in a larded lapwing, the lapwing in a plover, the plover in a red-legged partridge, the partridge in a woodcock - as tender as Mlle. Volnais - the woodcock in a teal, the teal in a guinea fowl, the guinea fowl in a duck, the duck in a fattened pullet - as white as Mlle. Belmont, as fleshy as Mlle. Vienne, as fat as Mlle. Contat - the pullet in a pheasant, the pheasant in a large duck, the duck in a turkey - white and fat as Mlle. Arsene - and, finally, the turkey in a bustard".

Prince Albert was patron of the great 1850 London Exhibition. The mayors of Great Britain and Ireland opened the exhibition with a banquet in honour of the Lord Mayor of London and His Royal Highness. At this meal, they served the "Hundred Guinea Dish" (so called because its ingredients cost the then staggering sum of 100 guineas), made up of choice morsels of all the birds served in the general menu. It included: the *noix* of 24 capons, 18 turkeys, 20 pheasant, 45 partridge, 100 snipe, 40 woodcock, and 36 pigeon, together with the meat of 10 grouse, 6 plovers, 36 quail, 72 larks and orlatans from Belgium. This was all topped with a garnish made of cockscombs, truffles, mushrooms, crawfish, olives, American asparagus, sweetbreads, *quenelles de volaille* and green mangoes.

FIT FOR A KING

The Frenchman Le Vaillant was both a passionate explorer and celebrated gastronome. Travelling in South Africa, his diary for one occasion records:

"My servants presented me at breakfast with an elephant's foot. It had swelled considerably in the cooking. I could barely recognise the shape, but it appeared so good, exhaled so inviting an odour, that I hastened to taste it. It was a dish fit for a king".

"Comfort in the gout", Thomas Rowlandson.

Looks can be deceiving: it's eating that's believing.
> - James Thurber, 1894-1961.

"We'll save the world with pecan ice-cream!"

ON THIS DAY IN MARCH...

13th March 1943

- The *New York Times* reports that U.S. airmen have developed an efficient way of making ice-cream: "They place ice-cream mixture in a large can and anchor it to the rear gunner's compartment of a Flying Fortress".

16th March 1851

- Death of Sylvester Graham, who had devoted his life to brown bread and published in 1837 a *Treatise on Bread-Making*. Graham Crackers, made with whole wheat, are still popular in the United States.

19th March 1955

- The title "oenologist" (one who studies the manufacture of wine) is officially recognized by law in France.

À LA TROYENNE

The Trojan Horse was supposedly a gift from the departing Greeks to the besieged citizens of Troy. Through it, however, the city was lost: it contained armed men who had thereby gained access to the city. Little did the Greek carpenters who made it know that their horse would give its name to one of gastronomy's greatest dishes, **pig** *à la Troyenne*. There are many recipes, but in essence the dish consists of a whole roast pig stuffed with hundreds of birds. At one of his lavish banquets, the Roman epicure Lucullus presented his guests with wild boar *à la Troyenne*: within the first was a second; within the second, a third; within the third were hundreds of tiny fig-peckers.

Meals have often changed the course of history. Napoleon, for example, was infamously uninterested in what or how he ate. He wolfed down whatever was to hand and often suffered, in consequence, from acute indigestion. This paralysed him on two of the most critical occasions of his life, the battles of Borodino (16th August 1812) and Leipzig (18th October 1813).

ÉPROUVETTES

Éprouvettes are dishes of acknowledged flavour and excellence, the classics of cuisine. The French have refined the experience of the *éprouvette* into the positive and the negative. A story of Cardinal Fesch illustrates the point. Finding he had to give dinner to several illustrious clerics, the Cardinal was relieved to learn that his chef had just taken delivery of two fine turbots, fish of great value and much esteemed. But what was the Cardinal to do? To serve both, he thought, would be excessive and yet to leave one would be wasteful. "Both shall appear", said his chef, "and both shall receive the reception that is their due".

At dinner, a splendid turbot was produced in due course and carried round the table by a footman to the approval of all present - the *éprouvette positive*. Carrying it to the sideboard, the footman was seen to lose his footing. The turbot was spilt on the floor - an *éprouvette negative* indeed. Snapping his fingers, the chef ordered the footman: "Bring another turbot". The *éprouvette positive* was restored.

A army marches on its stomach.
                    - Napoleon Bonaparte, 1769-1821.

The first experiment in refrigeration proves more
successful than Sir Francis Bacon had hoped.

ON THIS DAY IN MAR/APR...

20th March 1685
- Dr. Bachot of Paris publishes a medical thesis arguing that chocolate, and not ambrosia, must
have been the food of the gods.

21st March 1626
- Taking advantage of a heavy snowfall, Sir Francis Bacon decides to "try an experiment
touching the conservation and induration of bodies". He goes out, buys a chicken and stuffs it
with snow. He catches a chill in the process and dies of bronchitis two weeks later.

23rd March 1928
- Prince Curnonsky founds the Academy of Gastronomes in Paris.

The Chinese are immensely fond of eating dog. One dog's gourmet dinner calls for:

First Course

Shredded and stir-fried fillet of dog, with shredded bamboo shoots and black mushrooms, garnished with finely shredded lime leaves.

Second Course

Double-boiled soup of the bones, meat scraps, penis and testicles (provided that the dog isn't a bitch).

Third Course

Braised paw and muzzle, with sliced ginger in a brown sauce.

Fourth Course

Steamed ribs, cut in thick slices, sandwiched with slices of ham and black mushrooms, served hot in their own juices.

THE SHIELD OF MINERVA

The Roman emperor Vitellius ruled from 2nd January - 22nd December in 69 A.D. On one occasion he gave a banquet at which 2,000 fish and 7,000 game birds were served. He considered his greatest achievement a dish he called *Shield of Minerva*. The recipe called for pike-livers, pheasant-brains, peacock-brains, flamingo-tongues and lamprey-milt. These ingredients, collected from every corner of the Empire, were brought to Rome by relays of fast naval ships.

An unusual meal took place in Yorkshire twice every year between 1830 and 1865. Charles Waterton was the eccentric squire of Walton Hall near Wakefield. In a grotto in his park, he had to dinner biannually 100 lunatics from the local mental asylum.

"The brilliants", Thomas Rowlandson.

No man can be wise on an empty stomach.
            - George Eliot, 1819-80.

"Could you open a little wider, Mr. Ronay?"

ON THIS DAY IN APRIL...

1st April 1564
- King Charles IX of France changes the beginning of the year from 1st April to 1st January. The French resent this change, and in protest begin to send each other worthless gifts on 1st April. Sweetmeats in the shape of fish are a favourite, because the sun was then in the constellation of Pisces.

5th April 1993
- The distinguished food and restaurant critic Egon Ronay insures his taste buds at Lloyds' for £250,000.

5th April 1930
- Mahatma Gandhi begins his Salt March and changes the face of Indian history.

Food is used primarily as a way of bringing people together. It can also be used, however, as a means of setting people apart. Asking someone you rather dislike to dinner and then producing a simply filthy meal is as effective a snub as any. The technique is seen at its best in the hands of Rachel ____, the auburn-haired Edinburgh saloniste and socialite with houses in London, Worcestershire and Portugal. She is beautiful, rich, charming, intelligent and much in demand.

is that Rachel had also asked several of her high society friends, instructing them to ignore utterly the stranger in their midst and converse only amongst themselves.

Things got worse. For dinner's first course, Miss ____ produced mackerel paté and toast. This would have been fine, had the paté not been off, the toast three days old and thickly spread with margarine. The main course was pasta shells, so over-cooked they resembled porridge, and dressed

"The pretty hostess", Thomas Rowlandson.

On one occasion, she was being wooed over-vigorously by a wealthy London stockbroker. She fled to Edinburgh. He followed. He showered her with gifts and would not take "no" for an answer. So our intrepid heroine asked him to dinner. He accepted with alacrity. What he did not know

with a rancid sauce of peanut butter and tomato paste. Pudding was a tin, opened at the table, of creamed rice.

The company left early. Miss ____'s over-zealous suitor has not been heard of since.

*Cooking is like love. It should be entered
into with abandon or not at all.*
-Harriet van Horne

The game larder.

ON THIS DAY IN APRIL...

6th April 1509
- King James IV of Scotland passes a law against illegal salmon fishing, and makes a second offence a capital crime.

9th April 1850
- Death of Balzac, great French novelist and gourmet.

12th April 1656
- The Dutch declare exclusive rights to the world's cinnamon trade.

The ancient Greek Philoxenus of Leucadas devoted his life to the pleasures of the table. In order that he might be able to seize and devour burning hot roast meat as soon as it was placed on the table, he needed to get his hands and mouth used to great heat. He did so by regularly immersing his hands in and drinking boiling water. At his banquets, everything was served so hot that only he could eat.

Philoxenus began as a gourmet but became a gourmand. His constant desire was to have the neck of a swan so that he might enjoy the taste of his food for longer before it passed into his stomach.

James Fuller of Kent, who lived in the 18th century, was famed for his appetite. He regularly ate a whole roast sheep at a sitting, following that on one occasion with three dozen pigeons. Breaking his fast one day with Lord Wooton, he ate eighty-four rabbits and eighteen yards of black pudding. He lived to a great age.

"The parsonage", Thomas Rowlandson.

The Roman senator Apicius was a famous gourmet. When he was disgraced and stripped of his possessions he killed himself, rather than endure a simple diet.

A PASSION FOR ASPARAGUS

Bernard Le Bovier de Fontenelle (1657 - 1757) was permanent secretary to the French Academy of Sciences and an infamous glutton, despite living so long. He had a particular passion for asparagus. On one occasion he invited the Abbe Terrasson to dine with him and arranged for half the asparagus to be served with butter, which he preferred, and half with vinaigrette. Approaching the table, however, the Abbe dropped dead of apoplexy. Fontenelle immediately shouted to his cook: "Serve them all with butter, all with butter!"

Having eaten nothing else for three days, the Roman emperor Heliogabalus grew tired of *foie gras*. So he fed it to his dogs instead. He died assassinated in the latrines. Across his throat was the sponge used by the Romans instead of toilet paper.

I never see any home cooking. All I get is fancy stuff.
          - The Duke of Edinburgh, 1921-.

"I don't know what you're fussing about. You've only lost your comb. I've lost a kidney!"

ON THIS DAY IN APRIL...

16th April 1921
- Harry MacElhone, barman at Harry's Bar in Paris, invents and serves for the first time the cocktail Bloody Mary.

16th April 1978
- Baskin-Robbins produce an ice-cream sundae of 600 lb. of ice-cream, dripping with 34 quarts of chocolate sauce and topped with 153 ounces of chopped nut.

18th April 1576
- Catherine de Medici is taken ill, having eaten "too many artichoke bottoms and the combs and kidneys of cockerels".

BAD BEANS

The ancient Greek philosopher Pythagoras had a great aversion to beans and forbade his followers from eating them. When his city was attacked and his only escape was across a bean field, Pythagoras preferred to stay where he was and meet death.

His aversion to the humble pulse arose from his belief that in eating beans one was devouring one's own parents, thereby causing great disruption to the cycle of reincarnation. The ancient Egyptians thought much the same thing, calling the place where the *Ka*, the soul of the dead, awaited reincarnation the "bean field".

Many others have also objected to beans, if for less august reasons. The great Church father St. Jerome prohibited beans to the nuns in his charge on the grounds that "*in partibus genitalibus titillationes producunt*" - they produce titillations in the genitals. Eleven centuries later, the English writer Henry Buttes banned beans on the grounds that they cause "flatulencie, whereby they provoke to lechery".

The bean's infamous tendency to cause flatulence means that this fine food is denied to jet fighter pilots and astronauts. As a pilot flies higher in an unpressurised cockpit, his intestinal gas expands. At 35,000 feet, for example, it will be 5.4 times its volume at sea level. A meal of beans before a flight would mean agony, whilst to an astronaut it could mean death: a spaceman passing excessive wind in a space-suit would asphyxiate himself. So it was that a distinguished NASA scientist urged the selection of astronauts *"who do not normally produce very large quantities of flatus"* and selection criteria which would *"eliminate those candidates who demonstrate marked gastroenterologic responses to stress"*.

Farters and bean-eaters would prefer the edicts of the Roman emperor Claudius. After hearing about a man who endangered his health in an attempt to restrain himself, Claudius specifically legitimised farting at table, either silently or noisily (*"flatum crepitumque ventris in convivio"*).

"Effects of gluttony".

Woe to the cook whose sauce has no sting.
           - Geoffrey Chaucer, 1345-1400.

A sauce with a sting.

ON THIS DAY IN APRIL...

19th April 1950
- Gayelord Hauser publishes his book *Live Young, Live Longer*, in which he advocates natural unprocessed foods. It becomes an international best-seller.

21st April 1520
- Preaching a sermon against the evils of private hunting, Martin Luther sparks off the revolt of the Black Forest peasants.

24th April 1671
- Fritz-Karl Vatel, Steward to the Prince de Condé, commits suicide because the oysters he had ordered for that evening's dinner in honour of Louis XIV had not arrived. They do so fifteen minutes after Vatel's death.

In Israel, the ultra-orthodox Agudat Yisrael party tried recently to have banned the sale of pork to anyone but Christians. In protest, less strict Jews staged a demonstration - a free lunch of ham sandwiches. As one of their number explained:

"I've never touched pork, but once you let these Agudat characters into your sandwiches, they'll want to climb into bed with your wife as well".

BOARD FOR THE AFFAIRS OF SHECHETA.

NOTICE TO THE JEWISH PUBLIC.

NOTICE IS HEREBY GIVEN, that

selling meat on a Stall in Wentworth Street, DOES NOT HOLD the LICENSE of the Board and that all Meat, &c., sold by him is according to Jewish Law Trifa (מרפה) and prohibited to be eaten by Jews.

London.   190). Sivan 5661   **By Order,**
                                           M. VAN THAL,
                                           Investigating Officer

באָרד אפ שחיטה

נאטים צום אידישען פובליק.

עס ווירד היערמיט בעקאנמ געמאכמ דאם

וואם פערקויפמ פלייש אויף א סמאל אין ווענטוואָרמ
סם. האם ניט קיין לייסענס פון דיא באָרד אף שחיטה
אונד לוים דעם אידישען דין איז אין אלעם פליש א.ז.וו.
וואם ער פערקויפט מרפה אונ אידרען מארן עסנים עסעו
מ. וואן מהאל. אינוועסטכטינטינג: אפסער

לונדון סין תרס״א:

שריד ינואר ונקעאריא פאו אנא. ראבבינאטורים, א קאטערשל מברים.

Warning against trader in non-kosher meat, c. 1900.

EDIBLE INSECTS

Western cuisine is now more eclectic than it has ever been. At insects, however, western tastes stick. This is strange, since insects are commonly eaten and enjoyed all over the rest of the world. In north Africa, they love locust dumplings; in India, red-ant chutney; in Laos, water beetles in shrimp sauce; in South Africa, fried moth caterpillars.

Insects in our daily diet would make sense. Beef is only 20% protein, yet fly larvae are 63% and locusts 75%. Perhaps it won't be long before a cookery book with a title like *"Eat Insects and Save the World"* reaches the best-seller lists. Someone who would be pleased at such an event, were he able to be there, is the Victorian naturalist Vincent Holt.

Holt believed that our prejudice against insects is absurd. He thought woodlouse superior to shrimp. He considered grasshopper fried in butter with parsley "delicious". One of his sample menus was:

Snail Soup

Fried Sole with Woodlouse Sauce

Curried Cockchafers

Fricassee of Chicken with Chrysalids

Mutton with Wireworm Sauce

Cauliflower with Caterpillars

Moths on Toast

However strong, food taboos give way to a stronger force, starvation. When Leningrad was besieged by the Germans in the autumn of 1941, almost 3 million people were trapped and starving. They boiled up shoes and briefcases to make "meat jelly". They made bread of sawdust, cellulose and floor sweepings. They stripped off wallpaper and licked the dried paste from the walls. Some ate the wallpaper as well.

Better is a dinner of herbs where love is than
a fatted ox and hatred with it.
                              - Proverbs 15.17.

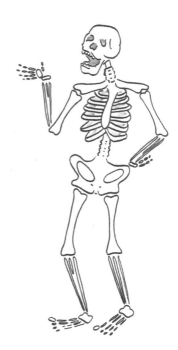

How best to dress bones.

ON THIS DAY IN MAY...

5th May
- Japanese Feast of the Banners (Nobori-no-Sekku) of paper carp, a symbol of health and longevity.

6th May 1681
- Denys Papin invents the first pressure cooker, announcing his discovery in a paper entitled: *How to dress bones and to cook all kinds of meats in a very short time and at little cost, with a description of the machine which must be used.*

10th May 1927
- By public referendum, Curnonsky (born Maurice Sailland) is crowned Prince of Gastronomes.

The Bemba tribe of Zimbabwe have a taboo against eating different kinds of food at one meal. They call this habit *ukusobelekanya*. Their meals always consist of a thick porridge *(ubwali)* made of millet and a relish *(umunani)*.

CONFUCIAN PHLEGMATISM

The Chinese are said to be the only people in the world with no food taboos. According to Jeremy MacClancy in *Consuming Culture*, they will eat "anything with four legs but a table and anything that flies but a kite". Yet when in 1885 the Chinese community of Tacoma in the United States invited local businessmen to dinner, they went to great efforts to avoid anything that might offend Western tastes. They failed.

One guest bitterly regretted the absence of shoulder of fricasseed rat from the menu and bemoaned the lack of:

"parboiled mouse, two months old, its teeth extracted, its tail pomaded with glue, its ears nicely set, the whole immersed in a sputtering crackling lake of dragon lard, dotted like an archipelago with ambrosial isles of waxed insects, tanned sealskins, swans' rudders, cormorant fillets and jackass corns".

The Chinaman who had organised the dinner replied with Confucian phlegmatism, "You win a few, you lose a few".

"Dinner party at a Mandarin's House", c. 1895.

The cook was a good cook, as cooks go, and,
as cooks go, she went.
                    - Saki (H. H. Munro) 1879-1916.

As good cooks go, she went.

ON THIS DAY IN MAY...

11th May 1911
- The first "all-soya" meal ever is served by France's Société Nationale d'Acclimatation.

11th May 1990
- One marzipan chocolate, weighing 1,850 kg., goes on sale at Diemen in Holland. It remains unsold.

12th May 1782
- Antoine Beauvilliers opens the "Grand Taverne de Londres", Paris' first great restaurant.

CANNIBALISM

In the western world at least, the greatest food taboo is against eating one's own kind, cannibalism. Shakespeare's *Othello* recounts amongst the many marvels of his life:

It was my hint to speak, such was the process;

And of the Cannibals that each other eat,

The Anthropophagi, and men whose heads

Do grow beneath their shoulders. This to hear

Would Desdemona seriously incline.

Anthropophagy from the ancient Greek for "man (anthropos)" and "eat (phag-)" has been used in English since the mid-16th century. **Cannibal** has a more interesting etymology, coming from the alleged name *Carib* or *Caribes* for one of the fierce and man-eating tribes of the West Indies. Christopher Columbus records the local Indian name for Haiti as *Caniba*. So, eventually, did "cannibal" come into English. By 1555, English writers record:

The wylde and myschevous people called Canibales or Caribes which were accustomed to eate manne's flesche (and called of the olde writers Anthropophagi) ... Vexed with the incursions of these manhuntyng Canibales.

By 1824, Prime Minister Disraeli was able to refer to the "political cannibalism of the mob". Some things don't change.

If it is not now much favoured in the west, cannibalism was widely practised by early man. Palaeolithic French cave drawings attest the fact. If not normal practice, it has long been adopted by the starving in war. When the Roman general Scipio eventually captured the town of Numantia in 133 B.C. after a long siege, his soldiers were horrified to find hidden in the clothes of dead women the half-eaten bodies of their children.

An interesting variant of cannibalism is **lycanthropy**. The word comes from the ancient Greek *lukos* for a wolf and *anthropos* for a man. So does it denote the power of a human being to transform himself into an animal, most commonly in folk-lore into a wolf. Many tribes in South America still believe that evil people often transform themselves into wolves. By killing and eating the wolf, the community destroys the malign spirit.

Cannibalism in Gabon District, Africa, c. 1908.

Open thine eyes, and thou shalt be satisfied with bread.
> *- Proverbs 20.13.*

"Please, just lay one more and I can have my papal pardon!"

ON THIS DAY IN MAY...

16th May 1568
- Pietrandea Mallioli of Sienna publishes the first illustrated book on mushrooms.

18th May 1869
- Hippolyte Mége-Mouriès invents margarine, after Napoleon III launches a competition to "discover a product suitable to replace butter for the navy and less prosperous classes of society".

19th May 1344
- The coronation feast of Pope Clement VI requires 3,250 eggs to make 50,000 tarts for the guests.

The oldest written recipe in the world, for a Chinese fish salad, comes from a book entitled *Yinshan Zhengyao*, (The Correct Principles of Eating and Drinking) by the Imperial dietitian, Hu Sihui, and dates to 1330 B.C. The salad comprised slices of raw carp, marinated in a mixture of radish, ginger, chives, basil and peppered knot grass. So there's nothing *nouvelle* about *nouvelle cuisine's* fondness for raw fish!

The only hindrance to rich Romans' appetite was capacity. So, by the reign of the emperor Nero, it became fashionable to employ slaves whose speciality was to tickle the back of your throat between courses. This was to make you throw up and ready for more. *"Vomunt ut edant, edant ut vomant"* - "They vomit to eat and eat to vomit", said the Stoic Seneca disapprovingly.

"Natives cooking locusts", c. 1860.

The pineapple contains an enzyme, bromelin, which can digest a thousand times its own weight in protein.

A ROMAN DELICACY

A great Roman delicacy was large white worms, specially bred in the hollows of trees. Dusted with flour, they were pan-fried, much as we treat whitebait, and served as an *hors d'oeuvre*.

A POISONOUS DELICACY

Perhaps the greatest delicacy of Japanese gastronomy is *fugu* (puffer-fish). It can kill you, containing in its skin, liver, intestines and ovaries *tetradotoxin*, a poison much deadlier than cyanide. Japanese chefs prepare very carefully transparent slices of the fish. As you eat, the tiny amount of the toxin makes your lips tingle. What if you eat just a little slice too much? What if the chef has misjudged? Three hundred Japanese a year can't tell you. They're dead.

In England there are sixty different
religions, but only one sauce.
                    - François Voltaire, 1694-1778.

"I haven't got enough flour left to powder my
wig, let alone bake a cake."

ON THIS DAY IN MAY...

20th May 1659
- David Chaillon opens the first chocolate house in Paris, on the corner of the Rues Saint-Honoré and de l'Arbre-Sec.

21st May 1775
- The *Guerre des Farines*, the Flour War, begins in France over the issue of taxation of wheat and flour.

27th May 630
- The Merovingian king Dagobert makes the grinding of corn a feudal right.

Sachertorte is a famous Viennese cake, first created at the Congress of Vienna in 1814 by the chef Franz Sacher, that caused great controversy. Sacher's descendants continued to serve Sachertorte in his restaurant after his death. They maintained that their cake, with two layers separated by jam and the top layer iced, was the real Sachertorte. Meanwhile, however, one Edouard Demel had begun to serve in his patisserie a Sachertorte made according to what he called the "true" recipe. His cake was covered with jam and then iced. The two families fought each other in court at vast expense for six years before the Sachers won. Demel responded by continuing to sell his cake, but as *Ur-Sachertorte*, the Original-Sachertorte!

In the global village, the distinctions of national cuisine are becoming blurred. A restaurant in Cincinnati recently advertised itself as:

"The Italian restaurant with the Spanish name hosted by the Jewish couple with the Greek partner featuring American steaks, French onion soup, Ecuadorian ceviche and Swiss fondue".

ON TRUFFLES

Truffles, either black (*Tuber melanosporum*) or white (*Tuber magnatum*) or black inside and white outside (*Tuber aestivum*), are literally worth their weight in diamonds. There are three principal producers, France, Spain and Italy. Each country produces approximately 50 tons of truffles a year. By comparison, world production of gold is approximately 1,500 tons and of platinum 85 tons.

The particular musky smell of the truffle is renowned. Scientists now think that this may be so attractive to human beings because it is caused by the same sex pheromone as men secrete in their underarm sweat!

It is that smell which pigs and dogs are trained to detect, leading their masters to the treasure. A good truffle-dog changes hand for thousands of pounds. In the Italian village of Roddi, near the "truffle capital" of Alba, there is a training school for truffle-dogs. Mongrels are preferred to pedigrees.

A truffle hunter with dogs, Wiltshire, c. 1870.

It is wonderful, if we chose the right diet,
what an extraordinarily small quantity
would suffice.
                    - Mahatma Gandhi, 1869-1948.

"A toad-eater", Thomas Rowlandson.

ON THIS DAY IN MAY/JUN...

27th May 1907
- 250,000 French wine-growers demonstrate in Carcassonne against low wine prices, carrying banners which read "Beggars today, insurgents tomorrow".

3rd June 1910
- *Croque-monsieur*, a hot sandwich filled with Gruyère cheese and ham, is first served in a cafe on Paris' Boulevard des Capucines.

3rd June 1960
- An un-named gentleman pays £207,000 for the Berkeley Louis XV dinner service at a Sotheby's auction in London.

The English noun sycophant, a flatterer, has an interesting etymology. It comes from the ancient Greek word for fig. Figs were highly prized by the ancient Greeks and became a valuable commodity. Their export was strictly controlled and subject to a very heavy tax. So it was that inspectors, called sycophants, were appointed to ensure that no figs were exported without due tax being paid. The sycophants became notoriously corrupt, often denouncing people falsely, and the word passed into English as a toady or false flatterer.

The world's most expensive spice is Mediterranean saffron (*Crocus sativus*). It takes 96,000 stigmas and therefore 32,000 flowers to make a pound.

FEORM - THE FOOD RENT

In 6th century Anglo-Saxon England, the victuals payable by groups of townships (vils) on the Royal Estates were known as *feorm* or food rents. The rent per vil had to be enough to provide the King and his household for 24 hours. According to one such *feorm* which has survived, sixty landholdings or "hides" at Westbury on Trym were required to supply King Offa with two "tuns" of clear ale, one "cumb" of mild ale, one of British ale, seven oxen, six wethers, forty cheeses, thirty "ambers" of rye corn, four "ambers" of meal and six *lang pero*, whatever they were.

Few peoples have enjoyed eating dogs. The Romans, however, made an exception once a year to their abhorrence of dogmeat. In Rome's early days, the city was attacked at night by the Gauls who climbed the Capitol rock. The sleeping guard dogs failed to give the alarm. The Gauls were announced and Rome saved by the sacred geese instead. So began the custom of an annual feast at which boiled dog was served and a goose carried in triumph, to commemorate the negligence of the first and the service of the second.

The most expensive food ever known to be sold was truffles, retailing in January 1985 in the Hafr El-Baten market in Riyadh, Saudi Arabia at £400 for 100 grammes.

"College Dons" (inspecting turtles brought alive from the West Indies), Thomas Rowlandson.

Tell me what you eat and I will tell you
what you are.
 - **Jean-Anthelme Brillat-Savarin, 1755-1826.**

"Honestly, darling, I'm only following the recipe!"

ON THIS DAY IN JUNE...

6th June 1830
- The gardener Neumann perfects the technique of the artificial pollination of vanilla. A cutting from one of the plants he has grown is sent to Reunion Island.

7th June 1740
- The anonymous cookery book, *Cuisinier Gascon*, first appears. It contains such recipes as *veau en crottes d'âne roulées*, veal as rolled-up donkey droppings.

8th June 1867
- The "Dinner of the Three Emperors" - Alexander II of Russia, his son the future Alexander III, Wilhelm I of Prussia and Bismarck - is held in Paris.

Poppea, wife of the Roman emperor Nero, never left home without her retinue of 500 milking asses. Each day, she took a bath in their milk, believing that it would make her skin more supple.

A recent survey analysed the eating habits of Britons on holiday. One family of four, on holiday in France, had with them teabags, instant coffee, pot noodles, eight packets of cereals, eighteen tins of baked beans, fourteen packets of Angel Delight and four tins of rice pudding. They weren't going to risk any of that foreign muck!

The world's most prized condiment is *Cà Cuong*, secreted in minute amounts by Vietnamese beetles and fabulously expensive.

ON HINDUS AND SACRED COWS
Hindus believe that each cow has over 320,000,000 gods and goddesses packed into her body. Small wonder, then, that the cow is sacred. Old cows are cared for in special shelters. Asked to explain this, one Hindu replied: "Would you put your aged mother into an abattoir?"

*Print "A short horned heifer 7 years old".
Inscribed "bred and fed by Mr. Robert Colling
of Barmpton near Darlington in the County of
Durham etc., etc."*

It is good for man to eat thistles, and
remember that he is an ass.
                    - E. S. Dallas, Kettner's Book of the
                                    Table, 1877.

"Horatio, could I borrow your chewing gum? I
can't seem to keep my dentures in place."

ON THIS DAY IN JUNE...

9th June 1907
- 500,000 French wine-growers demonstrate at Beziers against low wine prices. President Clemenceau calls in the army, who merely join the demonstrators.

9th June 1956
- Horatio Adams, first manufacturer of chewing-gum, dies at the age of 102.

11th June 1539
- Publication of first cookery book in Britain by Sir James Elliott.

Food was an important force in the development of America's west, often in unexpected ways. Jane Barnes, a bar-maid of some beauty from Portsmouth, England was one of the first female Britons to emigrate to Oregon. Arriving there on May 17th 1814, she soon caused a stir. The local Indian chief Cassakas sought her for his wife, offering to send her "one hundred sea otters and a huge quantity of dried salmon to her relatives". He promised to make her "mistress over his other four wives" and said that he would "never ask her to carry wood, draw water, dig for roots or hunt for provisions". She had the chief's word that "she would always have abundance of fat salmon, anchovies and elk".

Miss Barnes was unimpressed. She replied that she did not want a husband with "a flat head, a half-naked body and copper-coloured skin smeared with whale oil". Perhaps she just wasn't hungry.

RECESSIONARY RECIPES

Even in the teeth of a recession, demand for cookery books seems insatiable. Pages and pages of recipes titillate a public most of which is either on a diet or has no time to cook. But should they be "**recipes**" or "**receipts**"?

Both nouns come from the Latin verb *recipere*, to receive. "**Recipe**" came into English first, towards the end of the 16th century, but meant a medical prescription. Abbreviated as "**℞**" it still does in fancier medical circles and is derived from the symbol "♃" for the Roman god and patron of medicine, Jupiter. It was the middle of the 18th century before "**recipe**" was used in English to denote the ingredients and method of cooking of a particular dish. In the interim, "**receipt**" was used for "**recipe**". Now a receipt is a recipe and a recipe is a prescription. As food, so changes language.

Indians in Caribbean enjoying their dinner, c. 1770.

Peace and happiness begin, geographically,
where garlic is used in cooking.
                        - Marcel Boulestin.

ON THIS DAY IN JUNE...

16th June 1873
- A large colony of Mennonite Russians emigrate to Kansas, bringing with them a variety of wheat known as "Turkey red". It becomes the dominant variety sown between the Atlantic and Pacific oceans.

16th June 1878
- William Campbell, a publican in Newcastle, dies weighing 53 stone 8 lb. He had an 85 inch waist and a 86 inch chest. He was said to have enjoyed his food.

23rd June 1665
- Publication of Robert May's *The Accomplisht Cook*.

The noun "diet" can mean many things. The Diet of Worms, for example, was not a particularly unpleasant form of forced feeding, nor a Roman delicacy but an assembly, a congress held at Worms. The most famous of these "diets" was in 1521 when Martin Luther was called before Charles V to defend his doctrines. In its modern sense, the word diet comes from the Greek *diaita*, meaning "mode of life". It has meant the restricted or considered intake of food since Chaucer and his 1386 *Nun's Tale*:

> **"No dayntee morsel passed thrugh hir throte... a tempree diete was al her physic".**

The first systematic account of a diet in Britain is that written by William Banting (1797-1878), a London undertaker. In his pamphlet entitled *Corpulence*, he records how he reduced his weight from 202 to 156 pounds.

Slimness was greatly prized among the fashionable young ladies of the 1920s and roaring 30s who were, nonetheless, expected to drink and eat well. The solution they often adopted was to swallow tape worms, widely available from apothecaries and chemists for the purpose, usually dusted with sugar.

DIETING LITERATURE

Nowadays, the diet industry has reached enormous proportions. Books on dieting are regular best-sellers. *The Pasta Diet* shows how you can lose weight by eating pasta galore and *The Calcium Diet* by doing the same thing with calcium. *The Eskimo Diet* is not an invitation to cannibalism, but a panegyric on fish oil. For those in a hurry, there is *High Speed Slimming*, written by one Judith Wills who is also the author of such classics as *A Flat Stomach in Fifteen Days* and *Size 12 in Ten Days*. Rosemary Conley's *Complete Hip and Thigh Diet* has already sold a staggering two million copies worldwide, perhaps on its assurance that "dieting has never been simpler - there's plenty to eat and no calories or units to count, just incredible results to enjoy".

"Tight lacing, a little tighter", Thomas Rowlandson

Let us eat and drink; for tomorrow we shall die.

- Isaiah XVII.13.

"Only another 3,000 feet to go!"

ON THIS DAY IN JUN/JUL...

28th June 1838
To celebrate Queen Victoria's coronation, the great chef Alexis Soyer serves breakfast for 2,000 people at Gwydyr House, the temporary home of the Reform Club.

29th June 1969
Thirty butchers in Scunthorpe, Lincolnshire produce a sausage 3,124 feet long.

3rd July 1836
Alexis Soyer cooks a *banquet de luxe* for the Ibraham Pasha and 150 of his closest friends.

For the credulous, diets might save the world, the whale, rare orchids in Azerbaijan and all known ills. In *The Green Age Diet*, for example, Rose Elliot argues (take a deep breath) that if we lived off grains, fruits and vegetables:

"there wouldn't be such need... to cut down any more rain forest for the purpose of producing beef. The pressure on our farmland would be considerably relieved, our rivers and streams would become free of nitrates and chemicals from agricultural run-off. People eating such a diet would become lean, fit and well, because it's the right diet for their type of body. Heart disease, **circulatory diseases, cancer and all the suffering which these involve would decrease, and maybe even become a thing of the past. Hundreds of millions of pounds would be saved every year on medical care..."**

So now you know!

A DEMOCRATIC DIET?

Of the two candidates for President of the United States in 1840, the Democrat William Henry Harrison claimed to be a "man of the people" because he preferred to eat "raw beef and salt". His opponent, the incumbent Republican Martin van Burren, was a man of "fancy French cooking" who had appointed a French chef to the White House.

Harrison won on the popular vote. But he died thirty-one days after taking up office. There's a moral there somewhere.

"Manners and modes",
Shepperson in "Punch"

Eat slowly: only men in rags
And gluttons old in sin
Mistake themselves for carpet bags
And tumble victuals in.
                - Sir Walter Raleigh, 1552-1618.

From "Comparative Anatomy", Thomas
Rowlandson.

ON THIS DAY IN JULY...

7th July 1877
- Dr. John Harvey Kellog, having lost interest in cereals, publishes a paper entitled *Nuts May Save the Human Race*.

9th July 1886
- 27 horsemen drive 43,000 sheep to market over the 40 miles from Barcaldine to Beaconsfield in Queensland, Australia.

12th July 1516
- The Duke of Bavaria publishes a *Reinheitsgebot* or Edict of Purity, according to which the only ingredients allowed in beer are water, barley, malt, yeast and hops.

CONSTIPATION, MASTICATION & MASTURBATION

Constipation is a subject of perpetual fascination to food faddists. As early as 1801, William Nisbet devoted a large slice of his book *On Diet* to the subject, arguing that:

"The different discharges from the body possess a material influence on the health ... The first and principal discharge is that from the alimentary canal, or by stool, by which is removed the thick feculent remains of the food. This discharge should regularly take place once a day, and for this purpose a habit should be established of bringing it on by custom at a certain hour".

This was advice, as we shall see, to which the English responded with enthusiasm.

Yet a greater prophet of the evils of constipation was the Cambridge University don Eustace Hamilton Miles who, early in the 1900s, argued that constipation poisons the whole body and depresses its spirits. Miles was particularly concerned with young boys. In *A Boy's Control and Self-Expression*, he maintained that constipation clogged the alimentary canal, making it press against the "tender seminal vessels."

Miles believed there were two cures: a simpler diet and more chewing - muscular mastication. A boy who chewed his food thoroughly would be cleaner and tidier, within and without. Mastication, as it were, not masturbation. Miles advanced his case in no less than 50 books and two nutritional journals, *The Eustace Miles Quarterly* and *Healthward Ho!*

*"The stern preceptor",
Thomas Rowlandson.*

At a dinner party one should eat wisely but not too well, and talk well but not too wisely.
                    - W. Somerset Maugham, 1874-1965.

"As you can see, Ladies and Gentlemen, this 135 year old antique is in perfect condition."

ON THIS DAY IN JULY...

14th July 1893
- The restaurant "Maxim's" opens in Paris' Rue Royale.

15th July 360
- Apronianus publishes a decree defining the attributes of the Roman butcher.

17th July 1823
- Donkin, Hall & Gamble can the first tinned food - roast beef. The can was not opened until 11th December 1958. The beef was in perfect condition.

MATUTINAL DUTIES

Eustace Hamilton Miles' views had their effect. In the 1930s, a prospectus for a preparatory school in Sussex boasted proudly:

"Every visit a boy makes to the lavatory is recorded in a book, which is regularly inspected by the Nurse who is, in this way, able to check this very important duty".

Even as recently as 1952, another preparatory school brochure records the "matutinal duties supervised by Matron" at exactly 7:55 am. It is of more than passing interest to think of the nation's young élite all doing their duty, pushing at the same time.

The masticators' influence was profound. Horace Fletcher, Miles' American counterpart, lived by the slogan "Nature will castigate those who do not masticate". Perhaps his technique worked. His stools, certainly, were remarkably odour-free. We know this because Fletcher used to mail packets of his stools to nutritional scientists all over the world in support of his views.

"Fletcherizing", however, never really caught on. All that chewing was just too anti-social. As one contemporary observed of these masticators:

"The best that can be expected from them is the tense and awful silence that always accompanies their excruciating tortures of mastication".

"A heavy eater", from Seymour's sketches.

*"How long does getting thin take?", Pooh
asked anxiously.*
                    - A. A. Milne, 1882-1956.

*From "Comparative Anatomy", Thomas
Rowlandson.*

ON THIS DAY IN JULY...

19th JULY 1926
- Dr. James Empringham publishes a book entitled *Intestinal Gardening for the Prolongation of Youth.*

21st JULY 1873
- The first consignment of frozen meat is shipped from Melbourne, Australia to England. It was rotten on arrival.

21st JULY 1835
- A patent for condensing milk is granted to Sir Charles Thomas Newton.

There are many occasions when Mr. Miles' advice on constipation might have proved useful. One such occurs in the Roman Petronius' novel **The Satyricon**. This satirises an elaborate dinner given by the *nouveau riche* businessman Trimalchio. He leaves the banquet rather suddenly. Returning, he explains to the company:

"Excuse me, gentlemen, but I haven't had a decent crap (***venter mihi non respondit***) for several days. All the doctors are puzzled. Still, I found pomegranate rind useful, and pinewood boiled in vinegar... I have such rumblings in my gut you'd think there was a bull there. So if any of you wishes to retire, don't be shy. I can't imagine any torture like holding oneself in... As far as I'm concerned, you may relieve yourselves here in the dining-room. The doctors are dead against holding it in. But if you feel a really big one coming on, everything is ready outside: water, towels and all the other little comforts. Take my word for it, vapours go to the brain and unsettle the whole body. I know many people have died this way, by refusing to admit the truth to themselves".

"Mixing the punch",
Thomas Rowlandson.

Omelettes are not made without breaking eggs.

- Maximilien Robespierre, 1758-94.

How to make an omelette without breaking eggs.

ON THIS DAY IN JULY...

22nd July 1791
- By decree of the Paris Commune, the royal gardens at Tuileries are turned into potato fields.

22nd July 1966
- Angus Barbieri of Tayport in Scotland ends a 382 day fast, the longest ever. He had survived on tea, coffee and soda water. His weight fell from 33 stone 10 lb. to 12 stone 10 lb.

23rd July 1850
- Baron Justus von Liebig, Professor of Chemistry at Munich, produces the first ever meat extract.

LAND OF COCKAGYNE

Socialists and intellectuals have **Utopia**. Those of religious bent have **Heaven**. Gourmets have the **Land of Cockagyne**.

This mythical place was defined by the late 16th century lexicographer John Florio as "the epicure's or glutton's home, the land of all delights". In Old French, *trouver cocaigne* is "to find the country where good things drop of themselves into the mouth". The origins of the word are obscure, despite Grimm's suggestion that it comes from the German *küchen* for "cake", because "the houses there were covered with cakes"! According to an early 14th century English poem:

Fur in see bi west Spaynge
Is a land ihote Cockagyne...
Ther beth rivers gret and fine
Of oile, melk, honi and wine
Watir servith there to no thing
Bot to sight and to waissing.

Not surprisingly, the Church disagreed. Apart from anything else, situated in the west Cockagyne was incompatible with Genesis ii.8: "And the Lord God planted a garden eastward, in Eden."

Yet the myth has lived on. As a child, I remember hearing a song called *The Rock Candy Mountain*:

"Oh the buzzing of the bees
In the cigarette trees
And the soda water fountain
And the lemonade springs
Where the bluebird sings
In the big Rock Candy Mountain.

In the big Rock Candy Mountain
You never change your socks
And the little streams of alcohol
Come a'tricklin down the rocks...

A lake of stew and of whiskey too
You can paddle all about 'em in a big canoe."

"A gourmand", Thomas Rowlandson.

*A true gastronome should always be ready
to eat, just as a soldier should always be
ready to fight.*
                    - Charles Monselet, 1825-88.

*From "Comparative Anatomy", Thomas
Rowlandson.*

ON THIS DAY IN JUL/AUG...

27th July 1966
- Death of Sakurazawa Nyoiti, founder of the Zen Buddhist macrobiotic diet.

3rd August 1585
- Catherine de Medici brings from Italy the first chef to the French court.

4th August 1991
- A cocktail of 1117.4 gallons of gin, lemon and orange juice, banana liqueur and grenadine is served at Benalmedena, Spain. The guests enjoy their evening.

Servants have long been as essential a part of formal meals as the food itself. The Romans in particular made a science of servants. They were never short of volunteers, for life as a domestic if enslaved servant was greatly preferable to, for example, working in a mine or as a gladiator.

A wealthy Roman household had the rank and duties of each servant clearly defined. The *obsonatores* did the shopping, buying in Rome's great markets the meat, fruit and many delicacies that even the most mundane Roman meal required. In the days before Her Majesty's Mail, the *vocatores* carried the invitations to dine, received the guests and placed them at table according to rank. The *cubicularii* adorned, arranged and kept in order the table-couches. Next *dapiferi* brought the dishes into the dining-room and the *nomenculatores* informed the guests of the names and characteristics of that of which they were about to partake.

Given the Romans' propensity for poisoning each other, the *praegustator* tasted each dish before it was served. The *structor* then arranged the dishes before the *scissor* cut up the meats. Young and dishy male servants, *procillatores*, served the guests and poured the wine. *Sandaligeruli* loosened guests' sandals and massaged their feet as they ate whilst *flabellarii*, equipped with peacock feathers, kept the flies at bay and cooled the room. When dinner was over, *adversitores* were on hand, their torches blazing, to escort guests home.

Overseeing all was the *triclinarches* or chief steward, patently a busy man. For behind the scenes he had another phalanx of servants to direct. The *lecticarii* carried the sedan chairs in which many guests arrived and left. The *focarii* cut the wood and kept the fires burning whilst many *scoparii* swept and cleaned and *peniculi* washed dishes.

So did many contribute to the often excessive pleasures of the few.

DOMESTIC SERVICE

Victorian England, however, was not much different. Even the moderately wealthy middle classes kept servants. In 1888, Mrs. Beeton's *Household Management* insisted that those with an income of £1,000 a year should have a cook, two housemaids and a manservant; those with £750 a year could do without one of the housemaids; with £300 a year, a cook and a housemaid were still possible, perhaps because their working week of six days from 5:45 am until 10:00 pm rewarded them, all found, with an income averaging £12 a year. Yet the 1931 census showed that there were still 1,142,655 females in domestic service in England and Wales.

"A large group of servants",
Thomas Rowlandson.

My wife and I tried to breakfast together,
but we had to stop or our marriage would
have been wrecked.
               - Winston Churchill, 1874-1965.

"The morning dram", Thomas Rowlandson.

ON THIS DAY IN AUGUST...

7th August 1801
- Joseph Berchoux publishes in four cantos the poem *Gastronomie ou l'Homme des champs à table*.

7th August 1848
- The return of Lord Hardinge, Governor-General of India, is marked by a banquet for 1,005 guests.

11th August 1868
- The restaurateur Louis Bignon is made a knight of France's Legion of Honour for services to gastronomy.

BOUNTEOUS BUTTER & MISERLY MARGARINE

Butter is splendid stuff, notwithstanding the fulminations of the health lobby, and essential to any gourmet. It has had its detractors before. Writing in 1655, Thomas Moffett described it as "the chief food of the poorer sort". But by 1855 it was back in fashion. Alas, the great cattle plague of 1865-7 caused a shortage of butter and drove up its price to one shilling and twopence a pound. Margarine, that product of a chemistry laboratory, came of age.

Its name comes, however inappropriately, from the Greek word for a pearl, *margaron*. Thus its pronunciation shouldn't be "marj-". Initially, its creator the French chemist Mége-Mouriès called it the uglier and more appropriate "oleomargarine" or, on a good day, "butterine". That led in Britain to the 1887 Margarine Act which set out, in essence, that butter is butter, not margarine. The original formula for making margarine involved heating to 45 degrees Celsius a mixture of finely minced beef suet, water, carbonate of potash and sheep's stomach.

Modern industrial production is no more attractive, but the marketing men have won the day despite such distinguished antecedents for margarine as this 1899 definition of margarine crystals:

"These are seen chiefly in putrid bronchitis and pulmonary gangrene".

Let the etymologist H.W. Fowler, writing in 1926, have the last word:

"Marj- instead of marg- is clearly wrong. It was nevertheless prevalent before the war, when the educated had little occasion to use the word".

"The finishing touch",
"Punch", 1894.

"Arf a pound of Margarine, please; an' Mother says will yer put the Cow on it, 'cos she's got Company!"

Provision faite en saison
Et gouvernée par la raison
Fait devenir bonne la maison.
(Seasonal produce and the use of common
sense make for a thriving household).
                    - Olivier de Serres, 1539-1619.

Demonstration of hygienic cookery at Rouen
University, 1885.

ON THIS DAY IN AUGUST...

11th August 1933
- En route to the Chicago World Fair for exhibition, "Big Bill", at 2552 pounds the heaviest pig ever, breaks a leg and has to be put down.

12th August 1966
- The Society for the Prevention of Alcoholism in Darwin, Australia is disbanded for lack of support.

17th August 1536
- King Francis of France decrees that anyone found intoxicated should be imprisoned on bread and water for the first offence; the second time, flogged in prison; the third, flogged in public and the fourth, have his ears cut off.

Toasts and graces are as old as drinking and eating. Before Dark Age man drank the health of the living, he drank the *minni* of the dead or of the gods. *Minni* is a splendid Old Norse word that means "love, memory and thought of the absent one". The European Middle Ages held their *minnying* or *mynde* days, a custom we might do well to resurrect.

Less positively, many cultures practised the custom of toasting as a check on poisoning. Your guest might be poisoning you, but if so he'd go too. We take the word "toast" from the Romans, who did a lot of toasting for both reasons. *Tosture* is Latin for "to scorch or roast". It passed into English because of the Roman habit of flavouring their wine with small pieces of spiced toasted bread.

THE EARLIEST ENGLISH TOASTS

William of Malmesbury, the early English chronicler, says that the custom of drinking a toast began in England with the death of Edward the Martyr. In 978, he was stabbed in the back while drinking a horn of wine which his mother, Queen Aelfthryth, had presented to him.

The Saxons were certainly great health-drinkers. In his *Historia Britonum*, Geoffrey of Monmouth says that Hengist invited King Vortigern to a banquet after which Rowena, Hengist's beautiful daughter, entered with a gold cup full of wine. Curtseying to Vortigern, she said "**Lauerd king wacht heil!**" (Lord King, your health). The king then drank and replied "**Drinc heil**". (Here's to you).

"The toastmaster", Thomas Rowlandson.

*Cauliflower is nothing but cabbage with a
college education.*
                    - Mark Twain, 1835-1910.

A cabbage with a college education.

ON THIS DAY IN AUGUST...

19th August 1790
- Riots break out in Saxony over the issue of game rights for all.

19th August 1905
- The Japanese scientist Ikeda announces the discovery of monosodium glutamate, extracted from the gluten of cereals, and now commonly used to add to the flavour of processed foods.

21st August 1962
- Van de Kemp's Holland Dutch Bakery of Seattle produces the world's largest ever cake, 23 feet high, with a circumference of 60 feet and weighing 25,000 pounds.

THE WASSAIL

A related custom is that of the **wassail**, from the Old English "**waes hael**", be whole or well. In *Sports and Pastimes of the People of England*, Strutt explains that "the wassail bowl, a bowl of spiced ale, was formerly carried about by young women on New Year's eve, who went from door to door in their several parishes singing a few couplets of homely verses composed for the purpose, and presented the liquor to the inhabitants of the house where they called".

Mediæval monks then took over the pagan wassail bowl, making of it the Christian *poculum cariatis* or loving-cup. At the Lord Mayor of London's banquets, the loving-cup is a silver bowl with two handles, one of which has a napkin tied to it. Two people stand up, one to drink and the other to defend the drinker. Having drunk, the drinker wipes the cup with the napkin and passes it to his "defender", whose neighbour rises to defend him. So is the cup passed round the room.

In different vein, Sir Richard Steele explained the practice of drinking toasts in the *Tatler* of 4th June 1709, recalling an event that had occurred in Bath some 30 years earlier:

"It happened that on a publick day a celebrated beauty of those times was in the cross bath, and one of the crowd of her admirers took a glass of the water in which the fair one stood, and drank her health to the company. There was in the place a gay fellow, half fuddled, who offered to jump in and swore, though he liked not the liquor, he would have the toast... This whim gave foundation to the present honour which is done to the lady we mention in our liquor, who has ever since been called a toast."

The custom soon caught on. By the 1850s, it was endemic. In *Memorials of My Time*, Lord Cockburn recalled:

"After dinner, and before the ladies retired, there generally began what was called 'Rounds' of toasts, when each gentleman named an absent lady, and each lady an absent gentleman."

Serenely full the Epicure may say - Fate
cannot harm me - I have dined today.
*   - Sydney Smith, 1771-1845.*

From "Comparative Anatomy", Thomas
Rowlandson.

ON THIS DAY IN AUG/SEP...

23rd August 1780
- Dr. Pegge publishes in London his cookery book *Forme of Cury*.

1st September 1689
- A decree of the French parliament allows grocers to manufacture as well as to sell sugared products, so ending two centuries of bitter dispute between French grocers and apothecaries.

6th September 1926
- Birth of Paul Bocuse, the great French restaurateur and gourmand, who becomes known as "primat des gueules (primate of the palate)".

ROUNDS

"Rounds" often continued until the company fell unconscious under the table. In his 1857 *Reminiscences of Scottish Life and Character*, Dean Ramsay recounts the experience of one gentleman, Duncan MacKenzie:

"He had been involved in a regular drinking party. As he marked companions around him falling victims to the power of drink, he himself dropped off under the table amongst the slain, as a measure of precaution; and lying there, his attention was called to a small pair of hands working at his throat. On asking what it was, a voice replied, 'Sir, I'm the lad that's to lowse the neck-cloths.'" (i.e. to untie the cravats of the guests and prevent their suffocation).

Or again:

"There had been a carousing party at Castle Grant. As the evening advanced towards morning, two Highlanders were in attendance to carry the guests upstairs, it being understood that none could by any other means arrive at their sleeping apartments. One or two of the guests, whether from their abstinence or their superior strength of head, were walking upstairs and declined the proffered assistance. The attendants were astonished, and indignantly exclaimed, 'Ach, it's sare cheenged times when gentlemens can gang to bed on their ain feet!'"

Toasts had long since not been confined to ladies. Many were general, like the beautiful Irish:

May the hill rise behind you,
And may the mountain be always over the crest;
And may the God that you believe in
Hold you in the palm of his hand.

Some toasts, though modern, have become timeless, like Humphrey Bogart's in *Casablanca*:

"Here's looking at you, kid".

The Roman toast of two thousand years earlier is as enduring: **"Bene vos, bene nos, bene te, bene me, bene nostram etiam Stephanium"**. (Here's to you, here's to us all, here's to thee, here's to me, and here's to our dear - woman of the moment).

"Drinking a toast",
c. 1830.

coldtonguecoldhamcoldbeefpickledgherkins
saladsfrenchrollscresssandwichespottedmeat
gingerbeerlemonadesodawater.
   - **A. A. Milne, 1882-1956, Winnie the**
Pooh.

From "Comparative Anatomy",
Thomas Rowlandson.

ON THIS DAY IN SEPTEMBER...

8th September 1944
- American cereal farmers celebrate the production of their billionth bushel.

12th September 1846
- First publication of Alexis Soyer's book *The Gastronomic Regenerator*.

12th September 1852
- The father of modern beekeeping, Lorenzo Lorraine Langstroth, announces a major improvement in bee hives: he has discovered the critical "bee space", a gap of 5/16th of an inch.

OF GOOD CHEER

The standard English toast "cheers" has interesting origins. The word came into English in the 13th century from the Anglo-Norman *chere* meaning "face", itself derived from the Latin for "face", *cara*. "Face" soon became a metaphor for the state of mind behind it, and hence "be of good cheer" or "cheers".

"Grace" means "giving thanks" and comes from the Latin *gratias agere*, to give thanks. In the earliest monastic refectories, each meal began with the words *Gratias Deo Agamus*, "let us give thanks to God." Long or short, graces continue to be said before and even after a meal. In polite German society, it is still customary before and after a meal to bow to one's neighbours and say *Gesegnete Malzeit*, "May your meal be blessed".

The giving of thanks at meal times has been a tradition in our universities since the foundation of the earliest college. The Scottish princess Dervorguilla, co-founder of Balliol College, Oxford ordained in the founding statutes of 1282 that *singulis etiam diebus, tam in prandio quam in coena, dicant benedictionem antequam comedant, et post refectionem gratia agant* - "every day both at dinner and supper they shall say a benediction before they eat, and after the meal they shall give thanks".

The custom of Latin graces has survived even the age of the microwave. Green College, Oxford, for example, founded only in 1979, uses the grace *Pro hoc cibo et sodalitate huius collegii te Deum laudamus* - "For this food and for the fellowship of this college we praise thee, O God".

THE GRACE CUP

The "grace cup" is a strange cross between a toast and a grace. It was begun by Margaret "Atheling", wife of the Scottish King Malcolm Canmore and a woman so devout that she was canonised. Driven to Scotland around 1069 by the Norman conquest, she found the restless Scots reluctant to stay at table for the grace *post cibum*, after the meal. So she arranged that a cup of the very finest wine should be passed round for all to drink, but only after grace had been said.

British officers drink a loyal toast at Sierra Leone on the Queen's birthday, 1889.

Nothing must disturb an honest man while
he dines.
              - Joseph Berchoux, 1768-1839.

"I told him it was sweet."

ON THIS DAY IN SEPTEMBER...

16th September 1542
- King Francois I of France is cured of depression by eating a dish new to France, yoghurt.

16th September 1888
- Edmund McIlhenny reports his discovery of the world's hottest spice, the capsicum hot pepper, on Avery Island, Louisiana.

16th September 1920
- Clarence Birdseye visits Labrador and observes how the Eskimos catch and freeze their fish. He returns to the US and invents a process for rapid freezing. The "Bird's Eye" company is born.

Most Britons have breakfast around 8 am, lunch between 12 and 1:30 pm and supper or dinner, even if they call it "tea", between 6 and 9 pm. It was not ever thus, nor is it so elsewhere. Go to dine in a Barcelona restaurant at 8 pm and you will probably find yourself alone - the locals won't start arriving until 10 pm.

THE ORIGIN OF LUNCHEON

Henry VIII had his main meal of the day at 11 am. Cromwell, however, dined at 2 pm. By the end of the 18th century gentlemen did not dine until 4 pm, having breakfasted after some hours' work at 10 am, and took supper around 11 pm. By 1815, dinner was later still and so began the custom of luncheon around midday.

Under Queen Victoria, afternoon tea grew in importance and the gastronomic day took on four fixed points. Working women stopped that one, even if a few grand hotels still serve proper afternoon teas for tourists and you still get cucumber sandwiches at a Royal Garden Party.

SHRINKING BANQUETS

As meals have moved, courses have shrunk. When the Prince Regent gave a dinner in 1817, there were a hundred courses. A hundred years later, guests at the coronation feast of George V enjoyed only eleven. When Elizabeth II was crowned in 1953, the banquet consisted only of four.

"The Waterloo dinner", Thomas Rowlandson

Greed is a passionate, reasoned and habitual
preference for those objects which flatter
taste.
  - Jean-Anthelme Brillat-Savarin, 1755-1839.

"Tythe pig", Thomas Rowlandson.

ON THIS DAY IN SEPTEMBER...

19th September 1528
- Canon Piero Valeriano is given haricot beans (*Phaseolus vulgaris*) by Pope Clement VII. He in turn gives some to Catherine de Medici as she is about to take ship from Italy to France. So does the haricot come to France.

22nd September 1900
- The world's largest banquet is held in Paris. France's 22,295 mayors are served by waiters who cover the 7 kilometres of tables on bicycles.

23rd September 1747
- A Prussian chemist, Andreas Marggraf, first extracts sugar from white beet (*Beta vulgaris*).

THE LANGUAGE OF LOVE

Across the world, the language of food is the language of love and sex. Pregnant women have a bun in their oven. Lovers might say "I want to eat you". A woman might say of a "sexy" man "what a piece of meat", whilst he considers her a "peach". Vulgar Frenchman do not seduce women, they fry them (*faire frire*) and put in the pot (*passer à la casserole*). Their verb *consommer* can apply both to meals and to marriage. In ancient Greek, the noun *parothides* means both "hors d'oeuvre" and "sexual foreplay".

The links between food and sex are old and well attested. In the 1960s and 70s, however, the hippie movement went further, turning oral sex into a literal feast. They would decorate their partners' "plate" with edible things like strawberry yoghurt and cottage cheese.

"A panting lover", Thomas Rowlandson.

In central Brazil, the Mehinaku tribe regard good sex, like good food, as *awirintyapai*, "delicious" or "succulent". Dull sex, like dull food, is *mana*, "tasteless". Sex with your spouse is often the latter but with lovers, they believe, the former. A gourmet, however, might prefer to agree with Talleyrand, for unlike libido the palate does not fade with age:

"Show me another pleasure which comes every day and lasts an hour".

How can one make friends without exquisite dishes? It is mainly through the table that one governs.
        - Jean-Jacques Camacérès, 1754-1824, when Napoleon ordered that the postal service should no longer carry food.

Gold prospectors' unsophisticated fare in a "hotel" at Symonstown, Transvall, 1887.

ON THIS DAY IN SEP/OCT...

26th September 1636
- The Catholic Bishop of Madrid publishes a quarto on the question: "Is it a mortal sin for a priest to drink chocolate before celebrating Mass?"

28th September 1684
- Nicolas de Bonnefons publishes his seminal cookery book *Les Délices de la Campagne*.

1st October 1945
- The U.N.'s Food and Agriculture Organisation (F.A.O.) is born.

Aphrodisiacs are a direct link between food and sex. Cleopatra, and she knew a thing or two, used pearls dissolved in vinegar. The Chinese preference for sea-slugs is more obvious: when touched, this beast with the shape of a cucumber swells up like a penis aroused. The Spanish dictator General Primo de Rivera, a lover of bullfights, used to eat warm and raw the testicles of the first bull killed in order to fortify his sex life. The comments of his mistresses are unrecorded.

For the age of cup-a-soup culture and the general drive towards instant gratification, there is the instant aphrodisiac. *Spanish Fly*, made from the dried blister beetle of southern Europe, will give you an almost immediate and violent erection of the clitoris or penis. It may well kill you too. But then, at least, you will be a fit subject for an interesting post-mortem.

COCKLE-BREAD
Englishwomen of the 17th century werc, for the English, atypically direct: they got their man by kneading a small piece of dough, pressing it against the vulva and then baking their "cockle-bread". In *The Merry Wives of Windsor*, Shakespeare's Falstaff has the general idea and lists for his lover the alleged aphrodisiacs of his day:

"Let the sky rain potatoes; let it thunder to the tune of 'Green Sleeves'; hail kissing-comfitts, and snow eringoes; let there be a tempest of provocation, I will shelter me here."

"A door way flirtation", Thomas Rowlandson.

There was an Old Person whose habits
Induced him to feed upon rabbits;
When he'd eaten eighteen
He turned perfectly green
Upon which he relinquished those habits.
                    - Edward Lear, 1812-88.

Sophie. 1993.

"Thank goodness eating is the
only exercise he takes!"

ON THIS DAY IN OCTOBER...

2nd October 1086
- William the Conqueror rewards his chief cook with a grant of land.

3rd October 1735
- "The Sublime Society of Steaks" is established by Lord Peterborough at Covent Garden, London.

5th October 1262
- The Emperor Barbarossa throws a tagged baby pike into a pond. Weighing 350 pounds, the same pike was caught and eaten in 1497, having lived for 235 years.

THE ANTITHESIS OF GASTRONOMY

Fast food is the antithesis of gastronomy, the province of the industrial chemist, not the cook. McDonalds sells more than 600,000,000 pounds of hamburger "meat" in its American outlets every year. Is it "meat"? Something like the following is involved in a Big Mac, according to Jeremy MacClancy:

Flake or grind 30 grams of beef shin (including gristle, sinew and fat). Mix this with 16 grams of beef mince, which includes heart, tongue and more fat. Add 19 grams of rusk and soya flour and 16 grams of beef fat. Blend with 20 grams of water, 2 grams of salt and spices, 1 gram of monosodium glutamate and half a gram of polyphosphates and preservative. Stir in 10 grams of "Mechanically Recovered Meat" which is actually slurry. Cook.

96% of all Americans eat this at least once a year. More than half a million Americans work for McDonald's at any one time. Since staff turnover is so high, by the year 2000 more than half of McDonald's customers will be former employees, even if they are not all graduates of the chain's educational institute in Chicago, Hamburger University, and Bachelors or Masters of Hamburgerology.

"A good meal",
Thomas
Rowlandson.

Gastronomic critics are as controversial as evangelists.
                        - James de Coquet, 1977.

From "Comparative Anatomy",
Thomas Rowlandson.

ON THIS DAY IN OCTOBER...

6th October 1790
- Jacob Schweppe announces the perfecting of an industrial process for making artificial mineral water. His descendants developed Schweppes Indian Tonic and Ginger Ale in the 1860s.

7th October 1643
- The cognac firm of Augier Frères & Cie is established, now the oldest in the world.

7th October 1897
- Mr. & Mrs. Bradley Martin throw the world's most expensive private party in the Waldorf Hotel, New York. It cost them $369,200 at a time when dollars were still made of gold.

THE CUISINE OF CLASS

Those parents, sadly few, who still defy microwaved TV suppers often despair of instilling tolerable table manners in their offspring. They should take comfort from the terrifying etiquette of Victoriana. It is worth quoting in its full awesomeness a passage from one of the period's books, the 1872 *Modern Etiquette in Private and Public*, in order that modern parents and their progeny might count their blessings:

"Very soon after the last guest has arrived, the servant ought to announce dinner and the host, after directing the gentlemen whom to take in, should offer his arm to the lady of the highest rank in the room, the gentleman of highest station taking the lady of the house...

The gentleman who takes you into the dining-room will sit at your right hand. Take off your gloves and place them on your lap. Before you, on your plate, will be a table napkin, with a dinner-roll in it; take the bread out and put it at the side of your plate. Lay the opened table napkin in your lap, on your gloves, and then listen gracefully, and with attention, to your companion, who will do his best to amuse you till the soup is handed round.

The lady of the house should be at leisure to give her whole attention to her guests. If a clergyman be present, he is asked to say grace; if not, the gentleman of the house does so.

The table is laid thus: in the centre is some exquisite ornament - an alabaster stand crowned with pineapples, beneath which hang clusters of grapes; or a frosted-silver tree, with deer etc., beneath it, holding on its branches glass dishes filled with the most picturesque fruit. Round it the dessert dishes are placed; then, small dishes of preserves, sweetmeats etc. At the house of a nobleman, with whom we occasionally dine, the table - a round one - is encircled by small silver camels, bearing on their backs silver baskets, holding tiny fruits or sweetmeats.

On each plate a bill of fare is placed, so that the guests may see what will be handed round, and may be prepared to select, or wait for, whatever dishes they prefer.

"The rout at the Dowager Duchess of Portland", Thomas Rowlandson.

If they will not eat, then let them drink!
**- The Roman admiral Publius Claudius,
commanding that the sacred chickens be
thrown overboard because they would not
eat the sacred barley.**

A Roman banquet.

ON THIS DAY IN OCTOBER...

10th October 1716
- The Marquis de Montrevel, a man famous for his courage on the battlefield, dies of fright when someone accidentally spills the contents of a salt cellar over him.

12th October 1743
- Mathew Daking, a sufferer from bulimia (a morbid desire to eat), is recorded as having eaten 384 lb. 2 oz. of food over the past six days.

18th October 1571
- King Charles IX of France publishes an edict that "no man engaged in the cultivation of land... for the sustenance of men and beasts" may be executed for debt.

Soup is then handed; wine is offered after it... Fish follows the soup. You must eat it with a fork, unless silver knives are provided. Break a little crust off your bread, to assist you in taking up your fish, but it is better to eat with the fork only, which you may do if it be turbot or salmon. Put the sauce when it is handed to you on the side of your plate.

After soup and fish come the side-dishes, as they would be called, if they were on the table - the oyster or lobster patties, quenelles etc.

Remember, that for these you use the fork only; as, indeed, you should for all dishes which do not absolutely require a knife. You must use a knife, of course, for cutlets of any kind, although they are side-dishes. It is proper to eat all soft dishes, as mince etc., with the fork only.

Do not put your hands on the table, except to eat or carve (the latter is not required at a dinner *a la Russe*). Do not use your handkerchief if you can help it; if you must do so, let it be as inaudibly as possible.

Meat, chicken or turkey are handed after the made-dishes. Then follow game, puddings, tarts, jellies, blancmange, etc.

For the partridge or pheasant, of course you use the knife and fork; all sweets are eaten with the fork, or spoon and fork, as you like; but the spoon is only required for cherry-tart, or anything of that nature, custard, etc.

Ladies scarcely ever eat cheese after dinner. If eaten, remember it should be eaten with a fork, not a knife.

You should never, by any chance, put a knife near your mouth."

"The servants' dinner",
Thomas Rowlandson.

The best therapy for all ills is good food.
                    - Leon Daudet, 1867-1924.

"The comforts of Bath", Thomas Rowlandson.

ON THIS DAY IN OCTOBER...

21st October 1811
- The American Benjamin Rumford announces his invention of the coffee percolator.

23rd October 1800
- Frozen meat, perfectly preserved, first reaches England from Australia on the ship *Strathleven*, fitted with a Bell-Coleman refrigeration machine.

25th October 1534
- Pope Clement VII dies, poisoned by eating inadvertently the mushroom death cap (*Amanita phalloides*).

THE YIN AND THE YANG

It is small wonder that it was easy to offend, that the Victorians seem too often overly concerned with form and not enough with substance. Still, it could have been worse. The Victorians could have been Chinese. Consider, for example, their rules for what you might think the simple matter of serving fish at table:

"If the fish is dried, turn its head towards the guest. If it is fresh, turn its tail towards the guest.

If it is summertime, turn the belly of the fish to the left; if it is winter, to the right."

The reason why: (which is more than the Victorians ever troubled to explain):

"Winter is the reign of Yin, not Yang, and Yin corresponds to the Below; the belly is seen as the lower part of the fish, and so is Yin. Moreover, during winter, the belly should be the best-nourished part, the fattest and most succulent. The belly is placed on the right-hand side since you should eat with your right hand and should begin by eating the best part of the fish. Since summertime is the reign of Yang, the rules are reversed."

"Chinese at Chow-Chow",
1857.

*Never get your meat from the same place you
get your bread.*
                    **- Groucho Marx, 1895-1977,
                       on office entanglements.**

*From "Comparative Anatomy", Thomas
Rowlandson.*

ON THIS DAY IN OCT/NOV...

4th November 1865
- Birth of Édouard Nignon, who is to become head chef to, amongst others, the Tsar of Russia, the Emperor of Austria and U.S. President Woodrow Wilson.

6th November 1492
- Anchored off the coast of Cuba, Christopher Columbus records: "This land is very fertile, and is cultivated with yams and several kinds of bean different from ours, as well as corn".

7th November 1944
- Told that the French were starving, Winston Churchill replies that a country with so many cheeses could never perish.

As it is to life, eating is vital to literature. Poetry and prose abound with descriptions of meals. In Keats' poem *The Eve of St. Agnes*, for example, there is a passage of which the advertisement for "Milk Tray" chocolates is but a poor derivative:

And still she slept an azure-lidded sleep,

In blanched linen, smooth and lavendered,

While he from forth the closet brought a heap

Of candied apple, quince, and plum, and gourd,

With jellies soother than the creamy curd,

And lucent syrops, tinct with cinnamon;

Manna and dates, in argosy transferred

From Fez; and spiced dainties, every one,

From silken Samarcand to cedared Lebanon.

Lord Groan's breakfast in Mervyn Peake's novel *Gormenghast* is rather different:

As he sat, this morning, in his high-backed chair, he saw before him - through a haze of melancholia that filmed his brain and sickened his heart, robbing it of power and his limbs of health - he saw before him a snow-white tablecloth. It was set for two. The silver shone and the napkins were folded into the shapes of peacocks and were perched decoratively on the two plates. There was a delicious scent of bread, sweet and wholesome. There were eggs painted in gay colours, toast piled up pagoda-wise, tier upon tier and each as frail as a dead leaf; and fish with their tails in their mouths lay coiled in sea-blue saucers. There was coffee in an urn shaped like a lion, the spout protruding from that animal's silver jaws. There were all varieties of coloured fruits that looked strangely tropical in that dark hall. There were honeys and jams, jellies, nuts and spices and the ancestral breakfast plate was spread out to the greatest advantage amid the golden cutlery of the Groans. In the centre of the table was a small tin bowl of dandelions and nettles.

"The interior of an inn", Thomas Rowlandson.

I pray that death may strike me in the middle of a large meal. I wish to be buried under the tablecloth between four large dishes.

- Marc Désaugiers, 1772-1827.

A gourmand.

ON THIS DAY IN NOVEMBER...

11th November 1474
- The Italian scholar Platina publishes his *De Honestia Voluptate ac Valetudine* (Concerning Honest Pleasure and Health), in which he argues that quality of food is more important than quantity.

11th November 1979
- Wild ginseng, the root of *Panax quinquefolium* and believed to have aphrodisiac qualities, sells in Hong Kong for $23,000 an ounce.

11th November 1385
- For the first recorded time, roast turkey is served at table during a banquet given by Philippe of Burgundy.

Bruce Chatwin's imagination is no less vivid in *The Viceroy of Ouidah*:

"Never, not even in the time of Dom Francisco, had Ouidah witnessed so unctuous a feast.

Pigs' heads were anointed with gumbos and ginger. Black beans were frosted with cassava flour. Silver fish glittered in a sauce of malaguetta pepper. There was a ragout of guinea-fowl and seri-flowers, which were reputed to have aphrodisiac properties. There were mounds of fried cockscombs, salads of carrot and papaya, and pastes of shrimp, cashew nuts and coco-flesh.

The names of Brazilian shrimps were on everyone's lips: *xinxin de galinha, vatapa, sarapatel, muqueca, molocoto*. There were phallic sweetmeats of tamarind and tapioca, ambrosias, bolos, babas and piles of golden patisseries.

Yaya Adelina, her head shaved and her cottons whirling with the rings of Saturn, lumbered round the table, scooping up a sample of each dish into a calabash carved with totemic animals.

Uncle Procopio moved towards the *petit-pains au chocolat* murmuring 'Byzance!' He had all but thrust one through his moustachios when Adelina slapped his back:

'Shame on you, sir! Eating before the Father eats!'

She set the calabash on a table outside Dom Francisco's bedroom window and covered it with a cloth of broderie anglaise.

Everyone waited for something to happen".

"Feasting", N. de Bruyn.

*In Scotland there is meat and drink enough
to give the inhabitants sufficient strength to
run away from home.*
                    - Samuel Johnson, 1709-84.

*From "Comparative Anatomy",
Thomas Rowlandson.*

ON THIS DAY IN NOVEMBER...

14th November 1662
- Henry Stubbe first publishes his treatise on chocolate, *The Indian Nectar*.

16th November 1271
- The brothers Polo and Marco, son of one and nephew of the other, leave the town of Lyas (now Iskenderum) in Turkey for Ormuz, where they first encounter a spice market.

16th November 1862
- The French courtier and gourmet Henri Vatel kills himself at table, in despair of the late arrival in a restaurant of a fish he had ordered.

A meal of a different kind is described in Isabelle Allende's novel *Eva Luna*:

Rupert, Brugel and their daughters were simple, lively folk with large appetites. Food was central: their lives turned around the labours of the kitchen and the ceremony of the table. They were all plump, and could not get used to seeing Rolf so thin in spite of their constant efforts to nourish him. Aunt Brugel had created an aphrodisiac dish that attracted the tourists and kept her husband inflamed. 'Look at him', she would say with the contagious laughter of a contented matron; 'he's steaming like a tractor'.

The recipe was simple; in a huge pot she browned onion, bacon and tomato seasoned with salt, peppercorns, garlic and coriander. To this she added, in layers, chunks of beef and pork, boned chicken, broad beans, corn, cabbage, pimiento, fish, clams and lobster; then she sprinkled in a little raw sugar and added four steins of beer. Before putting on the lid and simmering the stew over a slow fire, she threw in a handful of herbs grown in her kitchen flowerpots. That was the crucial moment, because no-one else knew the combination of spices, and she meant to carry the secret to the grave.

The result was a dark rich stew that was spooned from the pot and served in reverse order to its preparation. The grand finale was the broth, served in cups, and the effect was a formidable heat in the bones and a lustful passion in the soul.

"Family meal", Crispin de Passe.

*Dinner, the principal act of the day, can only
be carried out by people of wit and humour.*
                - Alexandre Dumas, 1802-70.

From "Comparative Anatomy",
Thomas Rowlandson.

ON THIS DAY IN NOVEMBER...

16th November 1987
- Bakers in Victoria, Australia begin making the world's largest ever Christmas pudding. When iced on 9th December, it weighs 3,064 pounds and 6 ounces.

21st November 1368
- Alfonso, King of Castile, issues a prohibition on any knight appearing before him within thirty days of having eaten garlic.

21st November 1991
- Joseph Neshoda gains ephemeral fame by paying £833 for a single glass of Beaujolais Nouveau in Toronto, Canada.

HUMBLE SODIUM CHLORIDE

Even in this faddist age of the "lo-salt" diet, salt is mighty important stuff. We would not survive without it. If the world's oceans dried up, we would be left with 4.5 million cubic miles of rock-salt. That is about fourteen and a half times the bulk of the entire continent of Europe above high-water mark. So we would all be covered in salt.

Humble sodium chloride, in one form or another, is fundamental to life. We need it as much as we do water, for it maintains the equilibrium of our body fluids. Man recognised this long before the 6th century Isodore of Seville argued that "Nothing is more necessary than salt and sun".

In *The Odyssey*, one of the earliest works of literature, Homer speaks with amazement of an inland tribe near Epirus who do not know the sea and use no salt. Others were more resourceful. The Roman historian Tacitus records how the ancient inland Gauls made salt of a kind by pouring brackish water over a wood fire and collecting the ashes.

It was perhaps salt's use as a preservative that made it so precious as man moved from being a nomad and became a pastoralist of settled community. Our prehistoric progenitors settled where there was salt in such places as Hallstatt in Austria's **Salzkammergut**. Its importance is regularly recognised in The Bible, where salt is a symbol both of incorruption and perpetuity:

"The Lord God of Israel gave the kingdom... to David... by a covenant of salt".
- *Chronicles II, 13.5.*

And so "to eat a man's salt" became a sacred bond between host and guest, as explained in Byron's poem *The Corsair*:

Why dost thou shun the salt? That sacred pledge,
Which, once partaken, blunts the sabre's edge,
Makes even contending tribes in peace unite,
And hated hosts seem brethren to the sight.

"Inside of a saltern at Lymington, with the manner of making salt", Thomas Rowlandson.

Fennel seeds when soaked in wine
Revitalize a heart that love makes pine.
                    - École de Salerne, 1500.

"Grog on board", *Thomas*
Rowlandson.

ON THIS DAY IN NOV/DEC...

22nd November 1493
- Christopher Columbus plants the New World's first orange tree on Hispaniola (now Haiti), having brought it with him from Lisbon.

27th November 1696
- The siege of Budapest by the Turks gives rise to the croissant: the Turks seek to capture the city by digging tunnels under its walls at night. The noise is heard by bakers, working at night, who raise the alarm. The Turks are repulsed and, as a reward, the bakers of Budapest are granted the privilege of making a special pastry in the form of a crescent from the emblem on the Turkish flag.

29th November 1620
- Wild turkeys save the colonists from the *Mayflower* from starvation and beget America's annual Thanksgiving.

EARLIEST TRADE

Salt was the reason for the earliest trade routes. So is it as important a part of human development as, say, fire or the wheel. One of Italy's oldest roads is the **Via Salaria**, by which the produce of the salt-pans of Ostia was carried to the peoples of the Etrurian plains. En route, the early salt merchants stopped at a certain staging-post on the river Tiber. So was Rome, the Eternal City, born from salt, just as Venice grew rich from the salt trade from around 800. The vast salt mines of northern India were worked long before Alexander the Great (356-323 B.C.) came upon them and formed the centre of a wide-spread trade. The caravan trade in the Sahara desert is still largely one of salt.

The use of cakes of salt as money is as old as history. Travelling through the east in the 13th century, Marco Polo recorded the use of salt as money as a custom of immemorial antiquity. The English word "salary" comes from the Latin **sal** for salt: early Roman soldiers were paid partly in salt, not coin. We preserve this in the English saying **"true to his salt"**, meaning "faithful to his employers".

Thus those of the "Don't Brigade" - those lobotomised joggers who say don't eat too much, don't drink, don't laugh, don't live and certainly don't smoke - who urge us not to eat salt should recognise the enormity of their suggestion. "If the salt have lost its savour, wherewith shall it be salted?" (Matthew 5.13)

Such people should certainly always be seated below the salt.

I am the Emperor of Germany, but you are
the Emperor of Chefs.
- William II to Auguste Escoffier, 1846-1935.

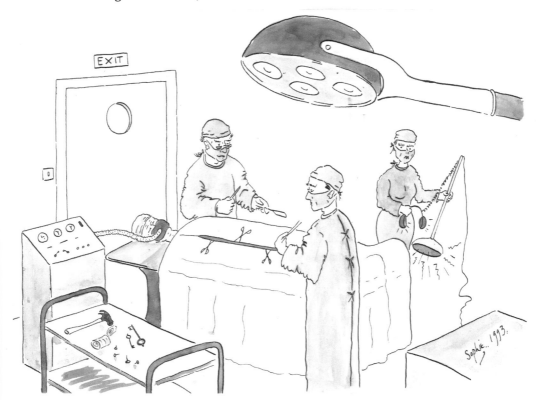

"Nurse, metal detector, please."

ON THIS DAY IN DECEMBER...

6th December 1960
- *The Journal of the American Medical Association* carries a report of compulsive swallowing. The patient's stomach contained 258 items, including a 3 lb. piece of metal, 39 nail files, 16 religious medals and 26 keys.

7th December 1782
- Monsieur de Nougarede publishes a book of 8,721 pages all about nougat. It has taken him fifty-five years to research and write.

10th December 1825
- The great gourmet Brillat-Savarin publishes, two months before his death, the book that is to make him famous despite its title: *Physiologie du goût ou Méditations de gastronomie transcendante, ouvrage theorique, historique et à l'orde du jour, dédié aux gastronomes parisiens par un professeur, membre de plusieurs sociétés littéraires et savantes.*

"If music be the food of love, play on", cries Orsino in Shakespeare's *Twelfth Night*.

Eating and drinking are intimately connected with music. **Spaghetti à la Norma**, for example, has nothing to do with Norma Major (even though she is said to enjoy both spaghetti and music) but with the Italian composer Vincenzo Bellini (1801-35). He came from Sicily. Sicily grows splendid aubergines that figure largely in **Spaghetti à la Norma**, a dish so much enjoyed by Signor Bellini that he named it after his opera *Norma*. That was almost inevitable: Bellini's fame had grown after his arrival in London, accompanied by the famous Italian soprano called Pasta.

Peach Melba is a rather different dish, eponomously named after its inventor Nellie Melba (1861-1931), the distinguished Australian soprano. She found that it soothed her vocal chords, failing which there was always **Melba Toast**.

The pudding **Pavlova** takes its name from the Russian ballerina Anna Pavlova (1885-1931), whose dancing was no less delectable. **Oeufs Bizet** and **Tornedos Rossini**, however, are surprisingly staid for two romantic composers. Which will live longer, their music or the dishes named after them?

Meals are much in evidence in opera. Act II of Verdi's *MacBeth* ends with the banquet that figures so largely in Shakespeare's play. Another banquet in his *Traviata* allows Alfred to insult Violetta most effectively. Mozart's great *Don Giovanni* ends with a memorable dinner party. In Puccini's *Tosca*, the villain Scarpia calmly eats his supper as he works his mischief before Tosca stabs him with the knife he has just used to peel an apple.

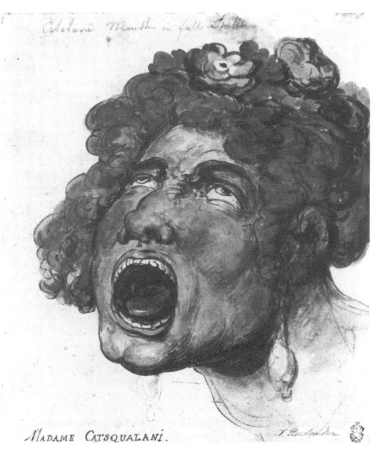

"Madame Catsqualani",
Thomas Rowlandson.

MADAME CATSQUALANI.

The two-pronged fork is used in northern
Europe. The English are armed with steel
tridents. But in France, we have the four-
pronged fork, the height of civilization.
                    - E. Briffault, 1846, Paris à Table.

"Tea on shore", Thomas Rowlandson.

ON THIS DAY IN DECEMBER...

12th December 1778
- Antoine Parmentier, the great advocate of the potato, publishes a paper entitled *Examen chimique de la pomme de terre*, in which he extols the potato's nutritional qualities.

15th December 1977
- Publication in the journal *Nature* of a paper entitled *Interparticle Forces in Multiphase Colloid Systems: the Resurrection of Coagulated Sauce Bearnaise*.

12th December 408
- Alaric, King of the Visigoths, enters Rome victorious and demands payment of 30,000 pounds of silver, 5,000 pounds of gold - and 3,000 pounds of pepper.

It is a sobering thought to consider, as you drink your cup of tea, that across the world 14,000 people are doing exactly the same thing each second. Tea is recorded as the elixir of immortality in Chinese texts as early as the 1st century B.C. By the 8th century A.D., the first technical and philosophical treatise on tea, the **Cha-Sing** or **Classic Art of Tea** by the Taoist poet Lu-yu was in wide circulation.

"Tea is not only the antidote to drowsiness", said the poet, "but one of the ways whereby man may return to his source".

Tea-drinking spread to Japan at the beginning of the ninth century. The tea ceremony became an important part of Japanese life, as it still is. Only five people may participate at one time, for like the fingers of the hand five is the symbol of union, of harmony and equilibrium.

It is the figure of "hierogamy", the marriage of the celestial principle (signified by the number 3) with the terrestrial (signified by the number 2) and, into the bargain, the symbol of yin and yang. It's all a far cry from Tetley's.

*Advertisement for tea -
not the recycled variety.*

Today Lucullus is dining with Lucullus!
**- The Roman general and epicure Lucullus,
106-56 B.C., reprimanding his cook for
preparing only a simple meal because there
were no guests.**

"I told you I've lost weight - 34 inches!"

ON THIS DAY IN DECEMBER...

23rd December 1775
- The French government announces that 100 million oysters have been gathered that year from the beds at Treguier and Cancale.

25th December 1870
- The restaurant "Voisin" offers a Christmas feast of the choicest meats from the Paris zoo: elephant consommé, civet of kangaroo, haunch of wolf with roebuck sauce and antelope terrine with truffles.

25th December 1967
- The U.S. circus fat lady Celesta Geyer announces that she has lost 28 stone in weight and that, from 79-84-84, her vital statistics are now 34-28-36.

WHEN TEA WAS CONTRABAND

As tea-drinking spread throughout the east, it remained unknown in the west until around 1560 when Venetian spice-traders and the first Europeans to visit China brought back bales of fragrant leaf. By the time of Oliver Cromwell (1599-1658), tea was sufficiently popular in Britain for the Lord Protector to impose a very unpopular tax on its import. The clergy led the way in importing tea illegally, hiding it in their church crypts where even the Roundhead soldiers hesitated to search. Drinking contraband tea became a way of signifying one's opposition to Cromwell and the drink's popularity was assured.

In 1700, England imported 20,000 pounds of tea. By 1800, the figure was 20 **million** pounds. In 1757, Samuel Johnson was able to record:

"A hardened and shameless tea-drinker, who has for twenty years diluted his meals with the infusion of this fascinating plant; whose kettle has scarcely time to cool; who with tea amuses the evening, with tea solaces the midnight, and with tea welcomes the morning".

Not everyone was pleased. In his *Cottage Economy* (1821), William Cobbett noted that:

"The drink, which has come to supply the place of beer, has, in general, been tea. It is notorious, that tea has no useful strength in it; that it contains nothing nutritious; that it, besides being good for nothing, has badness in it, because it is well-known to produce want of sleep in many cases and, in all cases, to shake and weaken the nerves".

Nobody listened. They drank more and more tea instead and still do, even if tea-pickers are no longer, as they had to be in ancient China, virgins aged less than 14 compelled to work in complete silence. Instead, we have the tea-bag and even, a sign of the times, instant soluble tea. The poet Lu-yu must be turning in his grave.

"A country fair", Thomas Rowlandson.

*Gastronomy has been the joy of all peoples
through the ages. It produces beauty and wit
and goes hand in hand with goodness of
heart and a consideration of others.*
                    - Charles Monselet, 1825-88.

PICKLED
ONIONS

PICKLED
WALNUTS

PICKLED
TETBURY
MAN

ON THIS DAY IN DECEMBER...

27th December 1968
- A man is carried unconscious from his kitchen in Tetbury, Gloucestershire. He is found to have 600 m.g. of alcohol per 100 m.l. of blood in his body. At the inquest, relatives describe him as a "fairly heavy drinker".

28th December 1982
- The famous Paris restaurant the "Tour d'Argent" announces that it has just served its 613,000th dish of *canard au sang* since 1890.

31st December 1600
- Queen Elizabeth I incorporates the East India Company by Royal Charter.

By comparison with tea, coffee, from the Turkish form **kahveh** or the Arabic **qahwah**, is a new boy. It was only around 1100 that Arabs in Ethiopia - the coffee tree is indigenous to Africa - began making a hot drink from pulverised coffee beans. Its popularity soon spread throughout the Islamic world. The first European to record an encounter with coffee was Prospero Alpina of Padua. Travelling in Egypt in 1580, he observed that:

"The Turks have a brew, the colour of which is black. It is drunk in long draughts, and not during the meal, but afterwards... as a delicacy and in mouthfuls, while taking one's ease in the company of friends".

THE COFFEE HOUSE

The drink reached England around 1630 where it, and the coffee houses in which it was served, were a sensational success. These coffee houses became the centre of society where men met to talk and plot and plan, not always to the pleasure of all. On the 23rd December 1675 King Charles II issued a "Proclamation for the Suppression of Coffee Houses" on the grounds that:

"Whereas it is most apparent that the multitude of Coffee Houses of late years set up and kept within this Kingdom... and the great resort of idle and disaffected persons to them, have produced very evil and dangerous effects... to the disturbance of the Peace and Quiet of the Realm; his Majesty hath thought it fit and necessary, that the said Coffee Houses be (for the future) put down and suppressed...".

. Poor Charles. The public outcry was so great that the proclamation was revoked on the 8th January. Coffee houses continued to thrive, as the poet Matthew Green, writing in 1731, attests:

Or to some coffee-house I stray,

For news, the manna of a day,

And from the hipp'd discourses gather

That politics go by the weather.

In the meantime, and before tea's popularity ousted coffee from its seminal place, the coffee houses had made at least one indelible mark on British society. In 1688 one Edward Lloyd had opened a coffee house in London where merchandise bound for the East and West Indies could be insured. So with coffee began Lloyd's, now the greatest insurance market in the world.

It was from another famous coffee house, the Great Piazza, that the playwright Sheridan watched in 1809 the fire at the Drury Lane Theatre saying: "A man may surely be allowed to take a glass of wine at his own fireside". One hopes that the theatre wasn't insured at Lloyd's.

"Coffee house in Salisbury market place", Thomas Rowlandson.

GLOSSARY OF TERMS

If you are already a gourmet, you'll probably know these terms, even if you don't understand them. People who work in smart restaurants use them all the time to impressive effect - until you see them reading *The Sun* or stretched out in front of *Neighbours*. For the aspiring gourmet, however, they are essential and should be much used in conversation, if not in cuisine - at least not all at the same time.

Agar-agar

- If asked, you should say "Don't you mean Bengal isinglass, alias Ceylon moss?" It's an extract of Indian or Pacific seaweed that binds everything together - cooks' superglue.

Aïgo boulido

- A garlic and water soup that gives rise to the saying: "L'aïgo boulido suavo lo vito (garlic soup costs friends)". The English equivalent is an Oxo cube with warm water.

Al dente

- Nowadays, at least in expensive restaurants, it means "raw". The dearer the food, the less it's cooked because there's a recession on and it saves on the gas bill. In its native Italian it means "to the tooth". Italians apply the term exclusively to pasta, perhaps because that's just about all they eat.

Allonger

- To extend an over-thick sauce. Gourmets use stock or wine. Scotsmen use water.

À l'américaine

- A way of ensuring that you cannot taste anything, it involves smothering chopped-up lobster with a sauce made from anything you have left over in the fridge.

À l'anglaise

- Whatever you're cooking, boil it to death, especially vegetables. If in doubt, fry it in used engine oil.

Analects

- The Greek and Roman slaves whose duty it was to clear up the remains of a meal. Their contemporaries are to be found sleeping near London's Embankment.

Antipasto

- What Italians eat when they want a change from pasta.

Attendu

- Well-hung. What the French say of a hare or pheasant hung for so long that its eyes drop out.

Barbouille

- Dracula's lips after a good nosh. Casserole a rabbit or chicken in red wine. Just before serving, pour in the animal's blood to give a thick smeary sauce. Not recommended for playschools.

Baron

- A joint of meat that includes the loins (the saddle) and both legs, so named by Henry VIII. England's only contribution to cuisine.

Béatilles

- Disgusting. Cocks' combs and kidneys, lambs' brains and testicles, diced foie gras and all that sort of thing all bound together with cream, stuffed into vol-au-vont cases and served at EEC summits.

Bisque

- Very expensive shellfish soup that is very cheap to make. Liquidise, shell and all, any mollusc, especially radioactive ones. Chuck in a little cream and a lot of spirit, preferably methylated. Serve.

Black Bryony

- Known in French as *herbe aux femmes battues* (battered wives' herb).

Blanc, à

- No longer acceptable as a culinary term, it used to mean cooking food without letting it discolour. Though still favoured in South Africa, western liberals prefer **blanc de noirs**.

Bleu, au

- Cooking fish by plunging it alive into a boiling court-bouillon. A flagrant violation of EEC directive 9,347,227.18.b.(m).

Bollito misto

- Literally "boiled mixed" and in its native Piedmont a stew of pigs' trotters, ox tongue, head of veal and anything else. Much favoured in fashionable London bistros as an obvious way of making money from the local fauna and flora.

Bourgeoise, à la

- A meal at which **serviettes** (q.v.) are used.

Brouet

- Any weak and disgusting soup or stew and the staple diet of the ancient Spartans. When a Spartan cook made it in Syracuse and the diners complained that it was inedible, the Spartan replied that its essential ingredients were missing - hunger, thirst and fatigue.

Buisson

- A fancy way of arranging food in a pyramid on a plate so that you are impressed by the appearance and ignore the taste.

Buvette

- A small bar set up in French law courts to sustain the judges. Nowadays they make do with hip-flasks.

Cannnelloni

- Big tubes for Pavarotti.

Capiltade

- A classic of French cuisine, this is a ragout (a stewed hotch potch) of leftover meats cooked until the whole thing disintegrates into a brown sauce. With added cocoa and sugar, it is served in British public schools as a pudding known as "Ganges' Mud".

Cévenole, à la

- Means anything with chestnuts in it, usually tinned. Why don't they just say so?

Chanoinesse, à la

- Terribly complicated; used to describe such dishes as baby carrots cooked in cream and then coated with a sauce made from sherry-flavoured veal stock. Dreamt up by church canonesses who had nothing better to do.

Chemise, en

- Full of chemicals.

Colcannon

- The zenith of Irish cuisine, it adds green cabbage to the standard meal of potatoes.

Colère, en

- A method of serving fish with their tails in their mouths. How sacked Chancellors feel.

Crécy

- Say "Do you mean Crécy-la-Chapelle (Seine-et-Marne) or Crécy-en-Ponthieu in Somme?", knowing that in either case it just describes any dish with carrots in it.

Débarasser

- In theory, this means "to clear away". In practice, it describes the process whereby cooked foods are dropped on the floor after leaving the cooker before being slapped on a plate and left to get lukewarm before they are served.

Dégorger

- The process of soaking meat and fish in cold water in a vain attempt to cleanse it of its accompanying steroids, colourings or radioactivity.

Duchesse, à la

- In Britain at least, an attempt to make horrible dishes look more appetising by surrounding them on the plate with piped and baked instant potatoes. A stock in trade of Rotary Club lunches.

Écossaise, à la

- Irish cooking at its zenith, it involves varying potatoes with oats.

Écuyer tranchant

- The flunkey responsible for cutting up the meat of French kings because they were so in-bred they were incapable of doing it themselves.

Émincer

- To cut anything edible and some that are not into thin slices, so saving food. Pretentious restaurants still do a lot of this with kiwi fruit.

En-cas

- What the French call a snack. What Brits know as a packet of crisps.

Faggot

- A deep-fried ball of minced pork and liver, cholesterol and hyper-tension.

Financière, à la

- You need to be an accountant, stockbroker or corporate lawyer to afford this garnish of cocks' combs, chicken quenelles, mushrooms and truffles, all bound in a Madeira and truffle sauce and covering, say, a baron of beef. It is said that Monsieur Attali, lately of the European Bank for Reconstruction and Development, is very fond of this dish, especially when he isn't paying.

Fond de patisserie

- Sweet-toothed.

Fondue

- Switzerland at its most imaginative.

Fructu, de

- A "bring a bottle" party. Originally a meal towards the cost of which all the participants paid a share.

Garum

- A condiment much loved by the Greeks and Romans, it was made by soaking fish guts in brine and was served with everything. The 20th century prefers tomato ketchup.

Gauloise, à la

- Any dish with a lot of cocks' combs and kidneys in it. The French are very keen on this sort of thing. They even named a cigarette after it.

Girolle

- What the French sometimes call a chanterelle, a kind of mushroom, when they're feeling cantankerous, which they usually are - unless they're eating.

Gnocchi

- If you're really smart, you will distinguish between various types of these small delicious dumplings, even if you don't know the difference: gnocchi *à la romaine*, *à la parisienne*, *à la piemontaise* and even *à la alsacienne*.

Gondole

- Those horn-shaped and ridiculous paper decorations much favoured at "silver service" rugby club dinners.

Gradin

- A tiered plinth, it's supposed to be made of edible substances and support others. These days, however, look out before you bite: it's more likely to be made of MDF (Multi Density Fibreboard), the same stuff that constitutes cornflakes.

Grand-duc

- A really expensive garnish for really rich accountants, stockbrokers and corporate lawyers. In essence, just smother everything with truffles and asparagus tips. Think of a price for the dish and treble it.

Gratin, au

- Allows the modern catering industry to re-heat dishes again and again.

Grecque, à la

- Cook anything anyway you like and cover it with buckets of rancid olive oil.

Grumeau

- A smart word for a "lump", as found in most peoples' white sauces and unwashed salads.

Hamburger

- A mixture of chemicals, soya meal, reconstituted meat, slurry, fat, gristle, flavouring, colouring, anti-oxidants and probably even **agar-agar** served by multinationals to the deranged.

Havir

- What the French call a dish whose outside has been seared. What most chefs serve burnt on the outside and raw on the inside.

Hot Dog

- America's second most important contribution to civilization.

Hôtelière, à la

- A dish served in a hotel that is **havir** and, usually, **au gratin**.

Hundred Year Old Eggs

- Widely available in most supermarkets.

Imam bayildi

- A Turkish dish of stuffed aubergines. It means "the Imam fainted" and is so called because one did once from sheer joy at the smell. Ex-President Jimmy Carter is said to have considered bombing Iran with imam bayildi smell capsules in order to free the American hostages.

Irish stew

- Potatoes, potatoes, potatoes.

Irridation

- The food industry's latest ploy to kill us all because they now own most of the country's crematoria.

Japonaise, à la

- The name given, logically, to any dish containing Chinese artichokes.

Jésus

- Testament to the sometimes warped proclivities of the Roman Catholic mind, this is a large sausage much favoured by born-again Catholics, adherents to Opus Dei and so on. It has a small wooden hook inserted in its end so that it can be hung up and smoked.

Jew's ear fungus

- All very odd. It's what Chinese restaurants in France call a blackish mushroom that grows on old tree trunks. There is certainly anti-Semitism in France, but amongst the Chinese?

Kedgeree

- The only positive result of the British occupation of India. The only positive case of Anglo-Indian integration.

Konbu

- Yet another of the interminable seaweeds that the Japanese eat when they're not eating whales' balls.

Knodel

- Yet more dumplings. But do you mean *markknodel*, *leberknodel* or even *zwetschenknodel*?

Landaise, à la

- Goose, goose and goose, inspired by the geese (sorry, cooking) of the Landes region of France.

Languedocienne, à la

- Served with masses and masses of aubergines or, when the genre is at its zenith, with masses and masses of goose fat.

Lavignon

- A bi-valve mollusc much enjoyed by the French and eaten raw or stuffed. It is harvested from sewage outfalls.

Limousine, à la

- In America, a take-away eaten in the car. In France, a way of preparing red cabbage. Elsewhere, something to do with bulls and artificial insemination.

Lumpfish

- A fish whose eggs, dyed, are mistakenly eaten as caviar at most smart bashes like Henley and Ascot, but not at EEC summits.

Macrobiotic

- A form of masochism which involves eating only wholegrain cereals and dried or raw vegetables. Although it comes from the Greek for "long life", most of its devotees don't get that far.

Magistère

- A concentrated consommé invented by the French gourmet Brillat-Savarin to combat "sexual exhaustion".

Maid of Honour

- As you would expect, an English tart.

Malakoff

- A sickly-sweet cake with a frothy filling, the term is more correctly applied to politicians than to gourmets.

Marinière, à la

- Encouraged by the EEC in the hope of reducing the European wine lake, it involves cooking mussels in white wine.

Mercédès

- The name for a type of garnish and a chicken soup, dreamt up by Frenchmen who could only afford Citroens.

Monkey brains

- One of the "eight treasures" of Chinese gastronomy.

Nantaise, à la

- As above, but it involves cooking white wine in white wine.

Naturel, au

- A polite way of describing the sort of food you get in British prisons and private schools.

Nouvelle cuisine

- Now old hat.

Oiseau sans tête

- Not in fact how you feel when you're cooking dinner for twenty, but the name for a slice of meat that is stuffed, rolled, tied (or even barded) and then braised. As you would expect, the Belgians make it sound very unattractive: *vogels zonder kop* in Flemish. They do it with sausages.

Oreiller de la Belle Aurore

- A pie created by the great French gourmet, Brillat-Savarin. It consists of chicken livers, young partridges, mushrooms, truffles, marinated veal fillets, slices of red partridge breast, white chicken meat and blanched calves' sweetbreads. It killed its creator's violin teacher. If you see it on a British Rail menu, order fish and chips instead.

Organoleptic

- The term describes the palatability of food. It is not applicable to that served on charter flights to Tenerife.

Orgies

- Discouraged by the British Medical Association, which recommends jogging in a nylon shell-suit instead.

Ortolan

- A diminutive species of bunting and great gastronomic delicacy. Gourmets cover their heads with a napkin when eating it, so as not to lose any of the aroma. The protection accorded this little migratory bird still doesn't stop thousands of Frenchmen from trying to ensure its extinction.

Pétéram

- Serve this to guests with whom you wish no further intercourse. It is a speciality of France's Luchon region in the Haut-Garonne and may explain why so few people ever go there. The dish is a stew of sheep's feet and tripe and calf's mesentery (the membrane covering the intestines).

Pets-de-Nonne

- Literally "nuns' farts", these pastry fritters are more respectfully known as *soupirs de nonne*, "nun's sighs".

Pluck

- The heart, spleen, liver and lungs of a slaughtered animal, it is said to be much favoured in certain Indian restaurants.

Poêlon

- A small saucepan whose long handle makes it popular with prima donna chefs who wish to throw things at their underlings.

Point, à

- In contemporary terms, when the microwave goes "Ping!"

Provençale, à la

- Anything cooked with lashings of garlic and olive oil like aïgo boulido (lots of garlic) and aïgo sau d'iou (lots and lots of garlic).

PTFE

- Or polytetrafluoroethylene, it is used to coat non-stick pans and mass-produced cakes.

Quadriller

- To mark the surface of grilled food with lines. What **nouvelle cuisine** chefs get up to when they think they've been re-incarnated as Pablo Picasso.

Rave

- Not a conglomeration of drugged and dancing teenagers, but the collective name for vegetables like turnips that are held in low esteem, except in Scotland where they form a welcome break from fish and chips.

Religieuse

- An outlandishly lavish and rich cake, so called out of respect for the austerity of the Holy Church.

Rösti

- After the cuckoo clock, Switzerland's second great contribution to civilization.

Russe

- A saucepan with an even longer handle than the **poelon** which chefs throw next. **À la Russe** is how you feel when it's hit you.

Sarladaise, à la

- Cooked in lots and lots of goose fat so that all you can see is - goose fat. The Danes go in for this sort of thing.

Serviette

- Never. Always and only a napkin, unless you're dining with John and Norma Major.

Soya

- Sold in Britain as mince.

Swimming Crab

- Often served in expensive restaurants because the meat is so damned difficult to get out of the shell that you order another stiff drink.

Table d'hôte

- What they call the canteen in the new privatised prisons.

Tartare, à la

- How cabinet ministers felt after disagreeing with Mrs. Thatcher.

Tartiner

- The French term for spreading something about.

Toad in the hole

- Britain's answer to *haute cuisine*, though one much objected to by The League Against Cruel Sports, the Ramblers' Association and so on.

Tokany

- Hungary's only dish not made exclusively from paprika.

Tortue, en

- Calf's head is usually served this way, once it has been twisted off. The dish, however, is conspicuously absent from eco-cookbooks.

Ulluco

- Attempts to introduce this South American tuber to Europe as a substitute for the potato have not been successful.

Vegans

- Fanatical nutters who may well be right.

Vert-cuit

- A posh way of saying "raw".

Vitamins

- Things taken out and then put back in by the modern food industry.

Welsh rarebit

- Getting rarer. It doesn't freeze or microwave well.

Worcestershire Sauce

- So called because its recipe was brought back to England from the East Indies by Sir Marcus Sandys, a native of Worcestershire, it is one of the few surviving relics of colonialism.

Ximenia

- The sort of incredibly obscure tropical fruit that pretty girls with too much make-up are always trying to sell you at supermarket check-outs. When offered a slice, children invariably say:

Yak, preferring sterilised, pasteurised and highly flavoured...

Yoghurt. But if forced to buy a ximenia, even at £6.52, you could always try putting it in your next dish of...

Zarzuela.

BIBLIOGRAPHY

The production of cookery books is one of Britain's few remaining growth industries, soon to be acknowledged by the appointment of a Secretary of State for Cookery Books. The Rt. Hon. William Waldegrave is widely tipped. Our bookshops burgeon with thousands of books, from which I have made the following selection as being of enormous interest but little use to a cup-a-soup culture. Many of these books even exist, and some can be found in such establishments as Simon Gough's splendid bookshop "**Food for Thought**" in London's Cecil Court. The aspirant gourmet, even if he or she knows nothing of these books, will pretend he or she does.

Anon:
THE PUBLICK-HOUSE-KEEPER'S MONITOR: Being a Serious Admonition to the Masters and Mistresses of Those, commonly called Publick-Houses, of what kind or Denomination soever.

J. Downing, 1730.

This small book should be introduced at once into the National Curriculum. Consider, for example: "..the [Publicans] are not ignorant that the scant measure is abominable, and yet it is to be found in most of their Houses .... they know well enough, tho' they are too often blind to the wickedness of it, that putting any guest into a damp Bed or Sheets, which has cost many a one his Life, is a Degree of Murder..." Some things don't change.

Barker, Lady:
HOUSES AND HOUSEKEEPING; A Fireside Gossip upon Home and its Comforts. William Hunt & Co., 1876.

Other classics to flow from Lady Barker's melifluous pen were *Station Life in New Zealand* and, for railway buffs, *Station Amusements*. One would of course expect nothing less from the Lady Superintendent of the National School for Cookery.

Commerell, Abbé de, and Lettsom, John Coakley:
AN ACCOUNT OF THE CULTURE AND USE OF THE MANGEL WURZEL, or root of Scarcity.

Translated from the French. J. Phillips, 1788.

A lot of people spent a lot of time considering the mangel wurzel - a kind of beet with a large root - as a cheap and hardy food for pigs, cattle and people of the lower orders. Gourmets have never taken to it. The whole thing is a muddle, anyway: somebody with a hangover in the 18th century gave "mangel wurzel" a spurious etymology from the German *mangel*, meaning "want" or "scarcity". That's absolute tosh - or so they say.

Cosnett, Thomas:
THE FOOTMAN'S DIRECTORY, and Butler's Remembrancer; or, the Advice of Onesimus to his Young Friends: Comprising Hints on the Arrangement and Performance of their Work; Rules for setting out Tables and Sideboards; the Art of Waiting at Table, and conducting large and small Parties; Directions for cleaning Plate, Glass, Furniture, Clothes, and all other Things which come within the Care of a Manservant, and Advice Respecting Behaviour to Superiors, Tradespeople, and Fellow-Servants. With an Appendix comprising various useful Receipts and Tables. Simpkin and Marshall, 1825.

This book was recommended reading for the Youth Training Scheme, but never really caught on.

Craig, Elizabeth:
THE ART OF IRISH COOKING.

Ward Lock, 1969.

This book is very short.

Dunlop, James Craufurd:
REPORT ON PRISON DIETARIES.

HMSO, 1899.

This considers, amongst other things, the advisability of half-starving prisoners. It is said to be much admired by certain Conservative MPs in the "No Turning Back Group", General Pinochet and other distinguished liberals.

Elliot, Robert H.:
GOLD, SPORT, AND COFFEE PLANTING IN MYSORE; With Chapters on Coffee Planting in Coorg, the Mysore Representative Assembly, the Indian Congress, Caste and the Indian Silver Question. Being 38 years' experience of a Mysore Planter.

Archibald Constable & Co., 1894.

Sadly, we no longer have the likes of Mr Elliot to bore for Britain. Contemporary politicians do it instead.

Fisher, M.F.K.:
A CORDIALL WATER; A Garland of Odd and Old Receipts to assuage the Ills of Man or Beast.

Faber & Faber, 1963.

The dust-jacket's copy-writer is right for once: "For many years Mrs Fisher has been collecting, from places and people all over the world, lore about restoratives and remedies - medicines, nostrums, herbs, oils, powders, charms, poultices, and miscellaneous cure-alls for coughs, colds, sore throats, freckles, warts, nosebleeds, insect bites, burns, rashes, rheumatism, excess weight, chills, fevers, indigestion, hangovers, impotence and wounds incurred in the mating season...".

Harvey, William:
THE FARMER'S WIFE.

Alex. Hogg, 1780.

Our progenitors took a strong line on sub-titles. You knew exactly what you were buying, in the days before perfidious copy-writers wrote gushing blurb for dust jackets. This splendid tome is sub-titled: **"Or the Complete Country Housewife. Containing Full and ample Directions for the Breeding and Management of Turkies, Fowls, Geese, Ducks, Pigeons &c., Instructions for fattening Hogs ... Ample Directions respecting the Management of Bees, with an account of the Use of Honey. To which is added The Art of Breeding and Managing Song Birds: Likewise a Variety of Receipts in Cookery, and other Particulars, well worthy the Attention of Women of all Ranks residing in the Country"**.

Hill, Benson:
The Epicure's Almanach; Or, Diary of Good Living; containing a Choice or Original Receipt or a valuable Hint for every Day of the Year. The Result of Actual Experience, applicable to the enjoyment of the good things of this Life, consistently with the Views of those who study genteel Economy.

How & Parsons, 1841.

Great stuff, this. Not the sort of book you will encounter at the General Assembly of the Church of Scotland. They're too busy making porridge.

Laird, A. Bonnet [Editor]:
RECIPES OF VARIOUS KINDS, in Cooking, Preserving, Brewing and other important Matters. Collected and

improved by An Amateur of the First Distinction, derived from Sources the most authentic, Ancient & Modern, Foreign and Domestic, and embracing a Compendium of useful and entertaining Knowledge.

Herbert Jenkins, 1927.

A bonnet laird, in Scotland, is a minor chieftain and not, contrary to popular belief, a form of haggis. This Mr A. Bonnet Laird, whoever he actually was, edited the manuscript of an earlier and interesting cook who, he tells us, amongst other things "leavened the mortar of her house with grated cheese".

Lison:
A polymorphism of the ability to smell urinary metabolites of asparagus.

British Medical Journal 281 (1980)

Several of the new NHS Trusts are rumoured to be considering the issue of this paper instead of sleeping pills as a cheaper and more effective cure for insomnia.

McGee, H. J., S. R. Long and W. R. Briggs:
Why whip egg whites in copper bowls? "Nature" 308 (1984).

Why indeed? One of the burning questions of our time, much addressed by President Clinton.

Rohde, Eleanor Sinclair:
HAYBOX COOKERY.

Routledge, 1939.

Invaluable for those trying to live on Supplementary Benefit.

Schaumburg, H. H., R. Byck, R. Gerstl and J. H. Masham:
Monosodium L-Glutamate: its pharmacology and role in the Chinese restaurant syndrome. Science 163 (1969).

Absolutely riveting.

Todd, P. H., Jr., M. G. Besinger and T. Biftu: Determination of pungency due to capsicum by gas-liquid chromatography. Journal of Food Science 42 (1977).

Quite.

Walker, J:
Physics and chemistry of the lemon meringue pie.

Scientific American, June 1981.

This is the sort of thing American scientists do when they can't find a space programme to work on.

Ward, Edmund:
A VADE-MECUM FOR MALT WORMS; Or, A Guide to good Fellows. Being a Description of the Manners and Customs of the most Eminent Publick Houses, in and about the Cities of London and Westminster. With a Hint on the PROPS (or Principal Customers) of each House. In a Method so Plain that any Thirsty Person (of the meanest Capacity) may easily find the nearest Way from one House to another. Illustrated with proper Cuts. Dedicated to the Brewers.

T. Bickerston, 1866

Proof that, however worthy, CAMRA (The Campaign for Real Ale) is new wine in old skins.

Watney, J.:
MOTHER'S RUIN: A HISTORY OF GIN.

P. Owen, 1976.

Allegedly Denis Thatcher's favourite book.

White, Florence:
FLOWERS AS FOOD; Receipts and Lore from many Sources.

Jonathan Cape, 1934.

Invaluable for those failing to live on Supplementary Benefit.

INDEX

ACKNOWLEDGMENTS

Acknowledgements are all the rage. Authors thank their dogs for their unfailing support, the power companies for supplying the power to run the word processor; they thank the postman; they thank the manufacturers, distributors and vendors of one instant coffee or another, without which stimulant their work could not possibly have been written nor the world irrevocably changed.

This isn't that sort of book. Tolstoy was not on my left shoulder nor A. J. P. Taylor on my right. But I had fun. Amongst those who contributed to that and this, Valentine Dawnay introduced me to the cartoons of Thomas Rowlandson, Aidan Weston-Lewis helped with the picture research, Mary Miers pointed me in some excellent directions as did Richard Irvine, Mike Fluskey was unfailingly helpful and efficient and Charles MacLean remained my dear friend, mentor and literary agent. I thank them.

Grateful acknowledgements are due for permission to reproduce the illustrations in this book:

The Antique Collectors' Club for permission to reproduce various Thomas Rowlandson drawings from their book *Mr. Rowlandson's England*.

The British Museum for permission to reproduce various Thomas Rowlandson drawings from *Comparative Anatomy* and *Caricatures, Volumes 1 and 2*.

The Huntington Collection, San Marino, California for permission to reproduce various Thomas Rowlandson drawings and sketches.

The Mary Evans Picture Library.

The Salisbury and South Wiltshire Museum for the picture on page 49.

The Ashmolean Museum for permission to reproduce the Thomas Rowlandson drawing on page 61.

...and especially to Sophie Drinkall for the cartoons on pages 12, 14, 16, 20, 30, 32, 34, 36, 38, 40, 42, 44, 46, 48, 52, 54, 56, 58, 62, 66, 74, 80, 86, 104, 108 and 100.

The Publishers would like to thank David Higham Associates for permission to reproduce the extract from Mervyn Peake's *Gormenghast* on page 95 and Jonathan Cape publishers for permission to reproduce the extract from Bruce Chatwin's *The Viceroy of Ouidah* on page 97 and Penguin Books for permission to reproduce the extract from Isabelle Allende's *Eva Luna* on page 99.